Communication in Interpersonal Relationships

SUNY Series in Human Communication Processes
Donald P. Cushman and D. Larry Kincaid, Editors

Communication in
Interpersonal Relationships

DONALD P. CUSHMAN
State University of New York at Albany
and
DUDLEY D. CAHN JR.
State University of New York at New Paltz

STATE UNIVERSITY OF NEW YORK PRESS
Albany

Published by
State University of New York Press, Albany

©1985 State University of New York

For information, address State University of New York Press, State University Plaza, Albany, N.Y., 12246

Library of Congress Cataloging in Publication Data

Library of Congress Cataloging in Publication Data

Cushman, Donald P.
    Communication in interpersonal relationships.

    (SUNY series in human communication processes)
    Includes index.
    1. Interpersonal communication. I. Cahn, Dudley. II. Title. III. Series.
BF637.C45C87 1984   302'.2   83-24228
ISBN 0-87395-909-4
ISBN 0-87395-910-8 (pbk.)

10 9 8 7 6 5 4 3

49,040

TO MY PARENTS EDWARD AND DOROTHY BAUMAN

AND

TO MY PARENTS, DUDLEY AND JEAN CAHN,
MY WIFE SHARON, AND DAUGHTER KATHY

Contents

Preface

The problem of communication in interpersonal relationships is a central theme of our age. Inquiry into the processes and problems involved in establishing, maintaining, and terminating such interpersonal relationships as those existing between friends, lovers, and mates has been the focus of numerous movies, television series, books, magazines, and newspaper articles. Many of these inquiries are based on myths, fantasies, or the exploration of non-traditional life styles. This book is an investigation of the traditional principles, processes, and skills involved in fitting together the separate lines of behavior of individuals into mutually satisfying interpersonal relationships through the process of communication. We focus upon the role human interaction plays in establishing, maintaining, and terminating those intimate interpersonal relationships which provide individuals with their sense of personal worth and relational satisfaction.

Four propositions underpin our attempt to provide unique insight into and guidance regarding the problems and processes involved with communication in interpersonal relationships. First, from a social rules perspective comes the proposition that human communication in establishing, maintaining, and terminating interpersonal relationships is guided and governed by socially established rules. The argument here is simply that such interpersonal relationships as those existing between friends, lovers, and mates are characteristic of human beings. Such interpersonal relationships are initiated, maintained, and terminated in and through human communication. Communication in such situations requires that the parties involved share a common code and interactional system. This common code and interactional system is conditioned by the normative rules of society which govern and guide the socially appropriate content and procedures involved in such interactions. Knowledge of the principles, processes, and skills involved in such human communication processes allows the parties involved to exert some influence over the outcomes of their interactions.

Second, from the symbolic interactionist perspective comes the proposition that who we are to others, our identity or self-concept, is a symbolic creation formed and sustained in our interaction with others. We are who we are because others in interaction support our attempts to be that way. If others choose to deny or ignore our attempts to be a certain type of person, then we can only be that way in our imagination. To be a self, to have a sense of identity, we must communicate and sustain that identity in interaction with others. It is the recognition of our identity by others that gives reality to the self, allowing for the initiation,

1

maintenance, and termination of interpersonal relationships with others. This, in turn, provides the individual with a feeling of self-worth and relational satisfaction or with a lack of it. Our self-concept or interactive identity is thus a communication rather than a psychological phenomenon, because it is interactively established and sustained. Knowledge of the principles, processes, and skills involved in the presentation, development, and validation of self-concepts allows the individuals involved to exert influence over their sense of personal identity and relational-worth.

Third, from an action theory perspective comes the proposition that our interpersonal relationships are constructed out of different types of reciprocal self-concept support. Action theorists argue that individuals exercise choice in the pursuit of goals and that one's choice of friends or mates depends upon selecting differential aspects of others' self-concepts and supporting those qualities. Such self-concept support is the chief ingredient leading to interpersonal attraction. Reciprocal self-concept support thus leads to mutual interpersonal attraction. Which qualities the individuals choose as the basis for mutual self-concept support, result in differential types of interpersonal relationships. Knowledge of the principles, processes, and skills involved in establishing, maintaining and terminating interpersonal relationships allows the individuals involved to exercise choice and control over their interpersonal relationships.

Finally, from a systems perspective comes the proposition that our self-concept, and in turn our interpersonal relationships, are significantly influenced by our participation in organizational, cultural, and cross-cultural interactional systems. Individuals are born into cultures, work in organizations, and meet individuals from other cultures. Each of these interactional systems exerts a significant and enduring influence on who we are and how we relate to others. Knowledge of the principles, processes, and skills involved in interacting in such systems allows the individual to exert influence over his or her presentation, development, and validation of self and interpersonal relationships.

It is in these four propositions that the potential for a unique insight into and guidance regarding the problems and processes of communication in interpersonal relationships resides. Chapter One examines communication as a major theme of our age and provides a unique conceptualization of human communication processes as dependent upon and manifesting respect for diversity and interdependence, as a basis for interpersonal, organizational, cultural, and cross-cultural relationships. Chapter Two explores the nature, function, and scope of individual self-concepts and the cueing, listening, and negotiation skills involved in asserting one's unique self. Chapter Three examines the processes involved in the presentation, development, and validation of individual self-concepts and the interaction skills unique to each of these processes. Chapter Four investigates the developmental processes involved in initiating and sustaining such intimate relationships as those required between friends and mates and the communication skills involved in influencing these processes. Chapter Five discusses the process of aligning sexual intimacy and emotional intimacy in interpersonal relationships by focusing on the problems encountered during this alignment and satisfaction it contributes to enduring interpersonal relationships. Chapter Six examines relational assessment and the communication skills involved in continuing, repairing, re-negotiating, and disengaging from interpersonal relationships. Chapter Seven in-volves an examination of how organizational communication influences the development, presentation, and validation of individual self-concepts, one's in-terpersonal relationships with supervisors and subordinates, and the skills involved in influencing job interviews and worker appraisals. Chapter Eight explores cultural communication and the role myth, ritual, and social drama play in balancing the individual and cultural influences on marital relationships, as well as the skills required of an individual to influence both traditional and non-traditional marital patterns in America. Chapter Nine discusses cross-cultural communication and the role it plays in forming friendships and mate relationships and in organizational communication between the Japanese and American people as well as the skills required for an individual to influence such relationships. Chapter Ten inquires into the future of a unique new type of relationship, that between one's self and the computer, by explaining the effects that man-machine interaction will have upon self, interpersonal, organizational, cultural, and cross-cultural communica-tion systems.

In short, this book attempts to explore the communication principles and the skills involved in influencing who we are in the presence of others and by extension how who we are influences the types of interpersonal relationships we form with others. This search is made by exploring human interaction in interpersonal, organizational, cultural, cross-cultural, and technological systems. While it is up to each of us as individuals to choose when and how we influence our relationships with others, it is in this vision of humankind as having the potential to function as active, intentional, reasonable, creative, and skilled influencers of our fate that the unique insight of this work resides.

1

Communication and its Role in Human Relationships

> Future historians who record what is being said and done today will find it difficult to avoid giving a prominent place to our preoccupation with communication. Communication does not signify a problem newly discovered in our time, but a fashion of thinking and a method of analyzing which we apply in the statement of all fundamental problems.
>
> Richard McKeon (1957:89)

A Major Theme of our Age

Almost as interesting as communication itself is the fact that people today are so interested in communication. The "problem of communication" is a major theme of our age. It fills our bookshelves and the advice columns of our newspapers. It spawns endless methods, therapies, and courses in the name of self-improvement, interpersonal adjustment, salesmanship, or whatever. It explains . . . and, we hope, solves . . . all other problems. If you want to find a mate, save a marriage, get a job, sell a used car, educate the public, prevent a war . . . then communicate!

Why have people recently become so interested in problems of communication? What set of forces or events has motivated this preoccupation? According to the distinguished philosopher, McKeon (1957), our preoccupation with communication today is not an accident, but rather a response to the convergence of four trends in contemporary society.

The first of these is a trend toward an increase in tolerance for cultural, group, and individual diversity. Young (1976), in his searching inquiry into the roots of contemporary pluralism, argues that "pluralism is a quintessentially modern phenomenon." In a country-by-country examination of the political forces at work in Asia, Africa, and South America, Young pinpoints "the pattern of social transformations which gave rise to the crystalization of cultural pluralism" (Young 1976:23–24). Whereas previous patterns of political identity were tied primarily to the nation state, Young argues that the emerging patterns of political identity are tied to a plurality of sources such as ethnicity, race, religion, caste, occupation, and geographic region. These diverse sources for group identity have created a cultural pluralism which subdivides nations as well as political, social, economic, and religious ideologies.

We can observe the manifestation of this increased tolerance for cultural pluralism in both the foreign and the domestic policies of the United States. Early in
this century respect for cultural diversity was low. This nation fought two world
wars in order to make the world safe for its culture . . . democracy. Democracy
was correct; other political alternatives were in error. By mid-century one specific
alternative . . . Communism . . . was viewed as satanic. The cold war of the
1940's and 1950's was witness to a lack of tolerance for global ideological diversity.
However, in the latter half of this century United States foreign policy has become
more tolerant of cultural and ideological diversity. United States *rapprochement*
with China and détente with the Soviet Union are indications of that change. The
United States' policy of non-alignment in Southeast Asia and the middle East offers
further evidence of a growing tolerance for cultural pluralism. Similarly, within
this country, Americans have witnessed an increased tolerance for group and
individual diversity. The Civil Rights movement of the 1960's produced two effects
relevant to our claim. The first was that it demonstrated to Americans the inhu-
manity of racial intolerance. The second effect was that the movement served as
a model for other minority groups: Mexican-Americans, American-Indians, Wom-
en's Liberation, and Gay Liberation, to name only four subsequent movements
aimed at establishing a group's subcultural identity within a broader culture. This
same tolerance extends to the realm of interpersonal relationships. People sometimes choose to associate with others who are quite different from themselves. A
recent field study of interpersonal attraction (Curry and Kenny 1974) indicates
that we may sometimes have as close friends individuals who think quite differently
from us and who do not see the world as we do.

A second trend recognizable in today's world is an increase in interdependence
both between and within cultures. The twentieth century has witnessed a rapid
growth in population throughout the world which has placed a serious strain upon
the world's resources. The unequal distribution of these resources has forced an
interdependence between cultures. Americans are in need of European manufac-
tured goods, Arab oil, and rare minerals found in Africa, Asia, and Latin America,
and the countries located on these continents are in turn in need of our food, arms,
and technology. America's national interests and goals can be achieved only with
the cooperation of other nations. Each culture is capable, if it withdraws its
resources, of inflicting serious harm upon other cultures.

Similarly we have witnessed a growth in interdependence between people within
the same culture. Industrialization, urbanization, and their companions, high specialization of function and strict division of labor, have made people within the
same culture interdependent in regard to goods and services. We live in nations,
cities, and families in which, respectively, a strike by airline employees, a boycott
by doctors, or a fight between family members can seriously impair our capacity
to pursue our individual interests and goals. Our interdependence and our diversity
require that we take account of others who frequently view the world in a somewhat
different way than we do. Our failure to take into account other people who may

differ with us in point of view will lead to the withdrawal of their cooperation and resources and the disruption of our capacity to achieve individual or group goals.

A third trend discernible in contemporary society is an increase in the availability of the means of communication. Increased access to the means of communication has made each of us aware of our diversity and our interdependence. *Television* has made most Americans as familiar with some of the attitudes, values and beliefs of Southeast Asians, Arabs, and Irish as they are with the opinions of their friends and co-workers. The mass media have familiarized us with the plight of blacks, Chicanos, and the poor. The *telephone* allows members of the same family to be scattered throughout the country and yet be able to maintain regular and close interpersonal contact. A conflict between members of the family in one part of the country is quickly transmitted to all other members of the family throughout the country. Because of this rapid expansion in the available means of communication, we have been thrust into a "global village" where we are confronted on a daily basis with individuals who follow different religions, pursue different interests, and view members of the same family differently, but with whom we must cooperate if we are to achieve our national, group, and individual goals.

A fourth trend present in contemporary society is an increase in the need to manifest respect for diversity as an antecedent for coordinated action. Why coordinate action? When individuals, groups, or nations are interdependent in regard to the solution of practical problems, their coordination is required in order to achieve mutually advantageous states of affairs. But when is coordination necessary? A coordination process emerges, according to Gauthier (1963), if and only if two or more individuals act in a manner determined by their mutual agreement. Coordination so defined depends not upon common goals but on agreement regarding the principles for guiding action. Agreement on the principles for guiding action is necessary to achieve mutual advantage. When two nations, groups, or individuals are interdependent and one of the participants fails to take into consideration the interests of the other, the ignored nation, group, or individual withdraws either its agreement or its participation in the interdependency until such interests are recognized by both parties. For example, the Arab oil embargo was provoked by the failure of the United States to take into consideration sufficiently Arab interests in dealing with Israel. Similar reasons have provoked various occupational groups to strike, racial groups to riot, social groups to demonstrate, and individuals to break off friendships. When are nations, groups, and individuals most likely to withdraw their cooperation? One answer is: at the moment when the larger community or individual fails to recognize an interdependent relationship, and fails to indicate, whether by recognition or concessions, the value of the contribution made by other groups or individuals to the interdependency. In such instances, this absence of recognition or concession provides the motivation to demonstrate interdependency by withdrawal of support. A withdrawal frequently prevents us from obtaining our desired goals and thus focuses attention on our need to manifest respect for each other as an antecedent to cooperation.

The preoccupation of people today with the problem of communication is no accident, but rather a response to the situations which confront us. When the problems we face are broad and complex, when the people capable of solving those problems have divergent and sometimes competing frames of reference, and when people require the cooperation of others for a satisfactory solution to their problems, then the initial distinctions necessary for examining problems as well as the means for achieving cooperation in the solution of problems must be found in communication (McKeon 1957). However, the growth in our tolerance for diversity and in our interdependence has placed stress upon the primary function of communication . . . namely, the motivation and coordination of collective action necessary for the solution of the common problems which confront interdependent groups. Communication aimed at motivating collective action in regard to our common problems depends on our establishing agreements regarding meanings, purposes, and values. Intolerance of diversity poses a substantial barrier to achieving the precise understandings and agreements on purposes and values necessary to direct and motivate collective action in regard to serious and complex problems. Such barriers frequently lead to confusion, misunderstanding, and insufficient understanding to motivate collective action. Yet the awareness of interdependence suggests that if an agent fails to recognize and manifest respect for others' interests, then those others will withdraw their support; the result will be a failure to realize goals. Such a failure will create a counter-pressure to enter into communication in such a manner as to understand where we differ, and to manifest respect for those others who have diverse interests and whose cooperation we need to achieve our goals.

The Need for a Paradigm Shift

The convergence of these four trends suggests a shift in our assumptions about the basic mechanisms that give efficacy to communication processes. Several implications can be drawn from our previous analysis for the construction of a new perspective on how effective communication proceeds.

First, the primary impulse for communication has shifted from persuasion and conversion to understanding and negotiation. Previously, communication arose from a desire to persuade or convert other people to our point of view as a prerequisite for the solution of problems. We wanted to persuade others to adopt our politics, religion, or values so we could do what a good Democrat or Catholic does. Coordination problems were problems of right or correct values: then the action to be performed was obvious given our common values . . . we elected Democrats, didn't practice birth control, and so forth. Solutions so located were optimal in their benefits from the point of view of both the interdependent system and the individuals who constituted it, because all participants shared a common set of values and thus employed similar criteria for evaluating results.

However, such conditions no longer should be assumed to obtain. In their place, the conditions of diversity and interdependence now give rise to the impulse to communicate. When our values and interests are no longer shared, the impulse to communicate accompanies a recognition that interdependent parties may possess differing conceptions of their mutual problems and find differing solutions desirable. Republican presidential candidates will need Democratic votes to be elected; therefore it is necessary to recognize the legitimacy of alternative conceptualizations of our national problems and through such an understanding to negotiate a solution which is beneficial to those alternative conceptualizations of the national interests. Solutions so located are almost always optimal for the system of interdependence, but suboptimal from each individual's perspective. The realization by diverse individuals that they are interdependent provides a pressure for locating and negotiating solutions which are the best they can do if they want the cooperation of others, but which are suboptimal in that these solutions are not normally taken if they had to consider only their own values and criteria for a beneficial solution.

Second, the efficacious use of communication has shifted from a reliance upon symbols which are value-laden in regard to a common value-system to a reliance upon symbols which are neutral in regard to diverse and sometimes competing value-systems. Previously, the effective use of communication was achieved by the use of value-laden symbols that were endowed with consensual meaning and motivational force because they were grounded in a common value system. Diversity and interdependence preclude such an approach. Value-laden symbols would introduce a whole array of prejudices in favor of one value system and give rise to a heightened awareness of diversity, thus generating disagreements and conflicts. Now, however, a symbol system is required which is more neutral in regard to the diverse and yet interdependent value systems involved, but which is endowed with consensual meanings and motivational force because participants engaged in a common task have found it productive for maintaining their interdependence, respecting their diversity and coordinating their joint actions.

Third, the conditions for the evolution and disintegration of communication relations have shifted from a focus on a recognition of our common values to a recognition of our interdependence. Previously the growth of communication relations began with an awareness of our common values and expanded in accordance with the recognition of the problems confronting those values; however, diversity and interdependence now preclude such a focus. In its place, the recognition of diversity and a heightened awareness of our interdependence now provide the basis for the growth of communication relations. The disintegration of communication relations results from a failure to recognize diversity and to see interdependence where it exists.

Fourth, the view of man as communicator has shifted from a passive responder to situational determinants to a purposive actor who intends and exercises choice when conveying and interpreting messages. Action theory provides a philosophical basis for understanding symbolic behavior. Action theorists write about intention, motive, reason, purpose, action, and events. Events (movements, motions) are a class of behavior that involves change. When observing events, one is able to identify three aspects: stimulus, response, and a causal relationship. The stimulus, which is referred to as a cause, is a physical change in the environment. The response, which is called an effect, is an automatic, immediate reaction to the physical change. It may be learned or unlearned. The relationship between the stimulus and the response is causal and requires a scientific explanation in the form of covering laws, commonly called physical laws.

Action theorists distinguish from events a different class of behavior called actions. Complex human behaviors, particularly social and communicative behaviors, exemplify members of this class. When studying the nature of actions, action theorists argue that it is impossible to identify causes, effects, and causal relationships. When actions occur, one is not likely to observe a physical change that functions as a stimulus or cause. Nothing functions as a response or an effect, because actions are arbitrary, learned, and often unpredictable. Since they are more complex than events, actions fail to conform to physical laws. They require teleological explanations in which intention and choice are employed to explain human behavior.

If action presupposes choice among goals and alternatives to these goals, how can one understand, explain, and predict human behavior? The answer lies in the study of rules, since they place constraints on the availability of choices. Rules are guides to action, norms, standards, and regulations. They function as criteria for choice among alternatives. Although rules represent social conventions which individuals and groups can violate or change, we suggest that when people know the rules they tend to conform to them.

A Multiple Systems Analysis

The purpose of our previous analysis has been to indicate why communication in general and interpersonal communication in particular can best be understood by describing the systems in which communication takes place. The concept *system* refers to a set of components which influence each other and which constitute a whole or unity for the purpose of analysis. To call a set of components a system implies that the components are organized in some way and that we are interested in the principles of organization or interdependence that make the whole work, rather than in the parts in their own right. It happens, however, that there are several points of view that one can take in describing the organization of a system. The three most important of these are function, structure, and process.

Simply defined, a *function* is something that a system does. More precisely, it is something that the system must do, in the sense that if the function were not performed the system would break down. Thus, respiration is a function of the human body; maintaining internal order is a function of a political system; and regulating the level of expressed affection is a function of an interpersonal relationship.

The *structure* of a system is the set of connections or relationships among its components. If a functional analysis answers the question, "What does the system do?" a structural analysis answers the question, "How is the system put together?"

These two questions are obviously closely related, in that what a thing does depends very much on how it is put together, and how we put a thing together depends on what we want it to do. Structure and function are just two ways of describing a single fact, a system's principal of organization. The structure of an engine is a set of components and mechanical linkages; the structure of a human relationship is a set of rules governing behavior.

The *processes* of a system are the changes which the system undergoes over time. This is a third way of describing the organization of a system. Here we describe the system as a temporal continuum or a sequence of events and become interested in how the system functions and evolves . . . how it responds by rule to situations which it assimilates to its structure, and how it accommodates or fails to accommodate to novel developments, thereby growing or decaying.

At the most basic level, what are the functions, structures, and processes of communication systems? We have argued that the contemporary problem of communication is how to ensure cooperation among people who are diverse in perspectives and interdependent in regard to the resolution of mutual problems. Following Cushman and Whiting (1972:219) we suggest that three propositions undergird that analysis: (1) that cooperative action is required to resolve common problems; (2) that communication facilitates cooperative action; and (3) that communication requires consensus upon communication rules. *The basic function of human communication in such a system is to regulate consensus . . . to adjust consensus to the need for coordination. The structure of a communication system is the set of rules which constitutes the consensus of the system at a given moment.* These rules are of two general types: code rules, which regulate the usage of symbols, thus structuring the content of communication; and network rules, which regulate the channels, circumstances, and manner of communication, thus structuring communication relations. To describe the structure of a communication system is to describe the set of rules which ensures coordinated collective responses in defined situations (if there is consensus on the rules). The process of human communication is to establish, maintain, and terminate relationships between people.

We find it both aesthetically pleasing and intellectually fruitful to think of human civilization as one great communication system. As we argued above, the people of the world have become interdependent; so the regulation of consensus on a worldwide scale has become a need . . . and, to some degree, an accomplished fact. If you accept the basic idea of a world system, then it is only a small step to think of that system as organized in hierarchical levels, as systems generally are. Within the great network there are clusters, and clusters within clusters, and so on. The structure of the world network is very complex, with clusters overlapping each other. For the sake of grasping the world intellectually, however, it helps to tidy things up by noting some clearly defined regularities in these multiple systems of communication. Table 1 presents the four systems and indicates how we distinguish between them from the standpoints of their communicative function, structure, and process.

Table 1
The Multiple Systems of Communication

Systems	Functions	Structures	Codes	Typical Processes
Cross-cultural	Consensus on recognition of cultural identity and interest	Multi-national institutions and communities	Diplomatic	Nation recognizes economic and cultural exchange
Cultural	Consensus about institutions	Nations, culture, class, sub-culture, region, community, family organization, group, role	Language, dialect, accent	Diffusion, especially via mass media; customs and rituals
Organizational	Consensus about production	Organizations, group, role	Jargon, technical terminology	Leadership, control, information exchange, bargaining, negotiation, discussion
Interpersonal	Consensus about self-concepts	Dyadic relationship within friendship, family networks	Personal style, personal reference	Development, presentation, and validation of self-concepts

Cross-cultural communication systems are, generally speaking, the broadest clusters in the world network. The basic function of such a system is to regulate consensus with respect to the recognition of cross-cultural identities and the co-ordination of a nation's political, economic, and social functions with other nations. The recognition of cross-cultural identities requires the cooperation of other nations as well as respect for the institutions and values which constitute that identity. Cross-cultural communication is the process by which an individual from one nation indicates to one or more other individuals from another nation the pressure of its cultural patterns on human behavior and seeks respect for and the cooperation of others in maintaining these patterns of interaction with other cultures. The *structure*-code and network values of cross-cultural systems are standardized through multi-national institutions and communities. The *communication processes* that typically occur at the cross-cultural level include: (1) world summits, meetings of heads of states, and military related treaties; (2) trade and economic negotiations; (3) international conflict and its resolution; and (4) cross-cultural exchanges of individuals be they performing artists, athletes, or tourists.

Cultural communication systems are, generally speaking, the longest-lived clusters in the world network. The basic function of such systems is to regulate consensus with respect to institutions . . . established values, beliefs, assumptions, expectations, and patterns of behavior. Institutions underlie the sense of unity that we feel with the other members of such networks as nations, regions, and social classes. People can identify with each other to the extent that they speak the same language, wear the same styles of dress, and support the same forms of government. The *structure* . . . code and network rules . . . of a cultural system is standardized throughout a nation, culture, subculture, social class, region, or community. The *communication processes* that most typically occur in cultural systems are: (1) the customs and rituals that are the concrete expression of institutions; and (2) processes of diffusion or the spread of ideas that change institutions or create new ones.

We add one final comment about the cultural level. In view of the above, we might reformulate the modern problem of communication as a problem of regulating consensus in a world where traditional institutions have broken down. Our identification within cultural systems has been weakened. There is less diversity among cultures as a world culture emerges, but more diversity within cultures as diffusion processes accelerate. As part of the same process, social, organizational, and interpersonal communications have increased in importance as bases for human cooperation. These shifts have made communication problematic.

Organizational communication systems, from a functional standpoint, are systems which regulate consensus with respect to production. People can cooperate in performing a task to the extent that each performs work that complements the work of the others. Thus, the focus of social organizations is upon the division of labor and the definition and performance of differentiated and integrated rules in the collective performance of some task. *Structurally,* such systems range from great, complex organizations like national governments and General Motors, to small informal groups working together to solve a homework problem or paint a house. The network rules of social organizational communication systems tend to be more formal (explicit) than those of a culture. Authority relations are especially important. With respect to code rules, a social organization tends to evolve a jargon or technical terminology having to do with objects important to the organization's task. The *communication processes* that most typically occur in social organizations include: (1) processes of leadership and control, such as orders, directives, and reports to superiors; (2) exchanges of information; and (3) formal and informal bargaining, negotiation, and discussion.

Finally, *interpersonal communication systems, functionally speaking, are systems which regulate consensus with respect to individual self-concepts.* A person's self-concept is the person's set of ideas about the kind of person that he or she is (Cissna, 1980, Cushman and Florence, 1974). Clyde considers himself an American, a bank teller, handsome, intelligent, a bad driver, quick-tempered, attractive to women, a joker, and fearful of snakes . . . these are all elements of Clyde's self-concept. The key points about self-concepts are two. *First,* unlike institutions and organizational roles, self-concepts are unique to individuals. *Second,* there is a mutual causal relationship between a person's self-concept and what others think of the person; a person's presentation of self to others, in other words, *affects* the impressions that others have of the person, and the reactions of others to the person in turn affect the person's conception of self. One's sense of self . . . both one's general sense of being a unique person and the more specific elements of the self-concept . . . depends absolutely upon participation in certain kinds of close, personal relationships with others. We call these interpersonal relationships.

The *structures* of an interpersonal system are not imposed from without, but emerge from the interaction of the people. The typical network form of an interpersonal system is the dyad (two people) within a friendship or family network. An interpersonal system tends to evolve a private code based on the personal styles and experiences of the individuals. The *typical processes* of interpersonal communication systems are those involving the development, presentation, and validation of self-conceptions. The individual in interaction proposes identities for self and other. The proposed conceptions are accepted or rejected by the other in a kind of tacit negotiation. By such processes individuals develop, present, and validate self-conceptions, creating thereby a relationship responsive to their needs . . . and needs responsive to their relationship.

The last point to be made about the multiple systems of communication is perhaps the most important, because it explains why we should be concerned with cross-cultural and organizational communication in what will be a theory of interpersonal communication. *The point is that the multiple systems are both mutually exclusive and interdependent.* On the one hand, defining the four systems helps us to understand what interpersonal communication is by contrasting it with what interpersonal communication is not. Given the definitions of the four systems, we ought to be able, in principle, to divide the content of any set of messages or the rules of any network into four groups: cross-cultural, cultural, organizational, and interpersonal. In that sense the multiple systems are mutually exclusive. On the other hand, understanding the multiple systems helps us to understand interpersonal communication because the four systems interpenetrate . . . they affect one another. Cross-cultural, cultural, and organizational systems constrain and influence interpersonal systems and vice versa. For example, the smooth working of an organization depends upon what is called the interpersonal climate . . . the quality of the personal relations between organizational members. Or again, marriage is a cultural institution, but marriage is also the formal framework for the most intimate of interpersonal relationships. In short, we cannot understand an interpersonal communication system without understanding its organizational, cultural, and cross-cultural environment. In the final analysis, the world network is all of a piece.

Some Implications

In conclusion, we indicate three significant implications of our analysis for the development of interpersonal communication theory and practice.

(1) We began by characterizing our modern world as containing people who are diverse, interdependent, and aware and who need to manifest respect for the uniqueness of others as an antecedent to coordinated action. The chief problem of communication in such a world is one of discovering and building upon areas of agreement in order to develop a consensus capable of guiding significant collective actions. The thrust of this argument within its interpersonal communication context is that if one is to form significant interpersonal relationships with others, one must first recognize the unique characteristics of others' self-concepts and manifest recognition and support for those others. Similarly, as the unique self becomes more and more free to vary, and this movement becomes more and more dominant in the behavior of individuals, then significant interactions with others will become less and less cultural and organizational in character and more and more interpersonal in nature. In the latter half of the twentieth century the problem of communication is in essence a problem of recognizing one's preferred cultural, organizational and interpersonal identity and then developing the communication skills necessary to give others the cue to that identity. The communication problem involved in establishing and maintaining interpersonal relationships is to relate people who are not sufficiently related by pre-existing organizational, cultural, and cross-cultural systems. Thus understanding the unique function (consensus about self-concepts,) the unique structure (dyadic relationships within friendship and family networks), and the unique processes (development, presentation, and validation of self-concepts) of interpersonal communication systems is responsive to its very core to the contemporary problem of communication.

(2) We have defined a system as a set of components that are interdependent and that constitute a whole or unity for purposes of analysis. The system perspective on interpersonal communication should be seen in contrast to the major alternative,

an atomistic perspective that views interpersonal communication strictly from an individual standpoint. This issue arose earlier in the context of characterizing our contemporary communication environment as made up primarily of diverse individuals who are interdependent with others for the solution of their mutual problems. We argued that the basic function of communication systems in such a context is the regulation of consensus. There we suggested that the consensus approach was useful because what was an optimal solution to a problem from the individual's point of view may not be optimal from the point of view of the system. Interpersonal communication involves more than just individuals; it involves individuals in a relationship. Furthermore, the relationship itself is always embedded in organizational, cultural, and cross-cultural systems. Tensions among the needs of the different systems sometimes create interesting problems. A woman may come to feel the need for a kind of independence that her relationship with a particular man from another culture does not allow. A pair of coworkers might want to develop an intimate relationship, but the conditions of their employment do not permit it. Thus, important problems of communication often arise because individuals, interpersonal systems, and other communication systems do not have the same needs. Similarly, a man may come to feel the need for a kind of interdependence that his relationship with a particular woman from another culture supports. A pair of coworkers may want to develop an intimate relationship which can only be supported by another whose employment is similar. Thus, important advantages to interpersonal communication arise because individuals, interpersonal systems, and other communication systems have similar needs. That this sort of analysis is possible would alone warrant a systems approach to interpersonal communication.

(3) Interpersonal communication is that communication which occurs in interpersonal communication systems. Interpersonal communication systems are distinguished from other communication systems in terms of function, structure, and process, but primarily in terms of function. Function is the leading aspect because communication systems, like naturally occurring, living systems are generally assumed to "work" in some way . . . the explanation of this is left to a theory of evolution. The basic function of such a system thus becomes a starting point, itself requiring no explanation, which can be called upon to explain other features of the system. In that sense, function explains structure and process. So interpersonal communication is first of all defined by its unique function, which is to regulate consensus regarding individual self-concepts.

The peculiar function of interpersonal systems implies peculiar needs by individuals for a recognition of diversity and interdependence in regard to individual self-concepts, the manifesting of respect for that diversity and interdependence, and then the development of some consensus regarding the character of individual self-concepts as a basis for establishing, maintaining, or terminating the structure of interpersonal systems. More specifically, we are suggesting that such social relationships as obtained between friends, lovers, and mates require the development of a consensus regarding the character of the individual self-concepts involved in such a relationship as a basis for establishing, maintaining, and terminating that relationship. In addition, we are indicating that such interpersonal communication processes as the development, presentation, and validation of individual self-concepts are necessarily involved in establishing, maintaining, or terminating such relationships.

An Overview of The Book

Thus, interpersonal communication is defined and warranted as a distinct field of study and practice by the unique function, structure, and processes of interpersonal communication systems. We feel that this way of distinguishing between interpersonal and other forms of communication raises a set of issues rich in implications for theory and practice. In the remaining chapters of this book we will introduce and explore these implications. More specifically, Chapter Two will explore the nature, function, and scope of the self-concept, indicate its dynamic character as a cybernetic control mechanism for human communication behavior, and discuss the communication skills which form the foundation for such controls. Chapter Three will explore the processes involved in the development, presentation, and validation of individual self-concepts, and explore the conception of communication competence suggested by such an analysis. Chapter Four will introduce self-concept support as the focal communication strategy in initiating and maintaining such interpersonal relationships as pertain between friends and mates. Chapter Six will explore the role of sexual arousal in confounding and/or enhancing interpersonal relationships. The reassessment of interpersonal relationships once established will be the focus of Chapter Six. Chapters Seven, Eight, and Nine will explore the influences of organizational, cultural, and cross-cultural communication systems on an individual's self-concept and interpersonal relationships. Finally, Chapter Ten will examine the effects of man-machine interaction on one's feelings of personal worth and relational satisfaction.

Interpersonal communication can thus be seen as an important area of study and practice with its own unique function, structure, and process and its interaction with other communication systems made clear. The systematic investigation of such an area will be guided by communication principles which allow for the improvement of human relationships in practice within interpersonal systems.

Propositions

1. Our age is characterized by interdependency, diversity, awareness, and a need to manifest respect in order to obtain the cooperation of others.
2. When heterogeneous people require cooperation between one another, then the initial distinctions necessary for examining problems as well as the means for achieving cooperation are found in communication.
3. The main function of human communication is to coordinate human activity through regulation of consensus with regard to some goals or tasks.

4. The multiple systems of human communication (cross-cultural, cultural, organizational, and interpersonal) may be distinguished on the basis of recurrent tasks, functions, and processes unique to each.

5. The function of interpersonal communication is to regulate consensus regarding individual self-concepts; the structure of such systems is the dyadic relationships within friendship and family networks; and the processes involved in such a system are the development, presentation, and validation of individual self-concepts.

6. Interpersonal communication systems may be affected positively or negatively by communication within organizational, cultural, and cross-cultural systems, and thus the intersection of such systems requires analysis.

Note

1. Portions of this chapter were previously published by Donald P. Cushman and Robert Craig, "Communication Systems Interpersonal Implications," in Gerald R. Miller (Ed.), *Exploration in Interpersonal Communication*, 5:37–58, Beverly Hills, California: Sage, 1976.

References

Austin, J. *How to Do Things with Words*. London: Oxford University Press, 1962.

Cissna, K. What is Interpersonal Communication? *The Communicator*. 52–63, Spring 1980.

Curry, T., and Kenny, A. "The Effect of Perceived and Actual Similarity in Values and Personality on the Process of Interpersonal Attraction" *Quality and Quantity*. 8:27–44, 1974.

Cushman, D. P., and R. T. Craig. Communication Systems: Interpersonal Implications. In *Explorations in Interpersonal Communication*, Vol. 5:37–58. ed. Gerald R. Miller, Beverly Hills, CA: Sage, 1976.

Cushman, D. P., and Florence, T. Development of Interpersonal Communication Theory. *Today's Speech*. 22:11–15, 1974.

Cushman, D. and Whiting, G. An Approach to Communication Theory: Toward Consensus on rules. *Journal of Communication*. 22:217–238, 1972.

Gauthier, D. *Practical Reasoning*. Oxford: Oxford University Press, 1963.

McKeon, R. Communication, Truth and Society. *Ethnics*. 67:89–99, 1957.

Miller, G. The Current Status of Theory and Research in Interpersonal Communication. *Human Communication Research*. 4, (2):164–179, 1978.

Searle, J. R. *Speech Acts*. New York: Cambridge University Press, 1970.

Wittgenstein, L. *Philosophical Investigations*. Translated by G. E. M. Ascombe, Oxford: Basil Blackwell Mott, 1953.

Young, C. *Politics of Cultural Pluralism*. Madison, WI: University of Wisconsin Press, 1976.

2

Interpersonal Communication And Individual Self-concepts

> From the symbolic interaction posture arose the idea that people develop and support their self-conceptions through interaction with others. In a segmentalized world, one in which diverse values and attitudes can co-exist, the particular shape of any individual's self-conception depends upon the particular individual from whom he develops them.
>
> A.O. Haller (1970:15)

A Symbolic Interactionist Perspective

In a world marked by an increased tolerance for cultural, group, and individual diversity and an increased interdependence both within and between cultures in regard to the solution of common problems, a particularly fruitful perspective for the development of communication theory is that of symbolic interactionism.[1] The symbolic interactionist perspective focuses on the processes involved in fitting together the lines of behavior of separate individuals into joint action through the transfer of symbolic information (Blumer 1966:540). If interpersonal communication is to be viewed as the regulation of consensus in regard to the development, presentation, and validation of individual self-concepts, the information one has regarding who one is can most productively be conceptualized as an interactive rather than a social or psychological construct. The information we have regarding who we are is *not* determined socially by whom others think we are, *nor* is it determined psychologically by whom we think we are. Rather, it is an interactively determined construct formed in interaction with others and based upon our own and others' communication skill in constructing and sustaining a consensus on an interactive conception of self (Cahn 1976). The communication processes involved in constructing and sustaining such a consensus are both complex and interesting.

First, our awareness of self arises from taking the role of others with whom we interact and asking what they must have thought about us in order to communicate with us as they did. *For example,* when others tell me that I am intelligent and aggressive what must they have been thinking about me to say that? In answering this question I must take the role of the other and look back at my own actions and communications and interpret their meaning from the others' point of view. *Second,* we may then decide that we need to assert various aspects of our preferred conceptions of self in order to influence others' perceptions of us. This action requires both some vision of what we would like to be perceived as and the communication skill to construct and sustain that vision from the others' point of view. *For example*, I may want you to see me not only as intelligent and aggressive but also as fair and friendly. *Third*, we need to recognize through interaction others' conceptions of themselves and the role their self-concepts play in either supporting or limiting our presentation of self. *For example*, others may feel that in order to be fair one must not be aggressive. This may severely limit my own ability to construct and sustain my vision of self as both an aggressive and a fair person. *Finally*, we need to realize that who we are in interaction, our self-concept, is a subtle interaction between our own desires and communication skills and the desires of others for us and their communication skills. *For example*, an individual's ability to manifest himself as intelligent may or may not be sustainable, depending on whether others (1) fail to challenge his assertion of self, (2) challenge and defeat his assertion of self, or (3) challenge but are overcome by his assertion of self. In short, our ability to create and sustain our vision of self depends upon the room others provide for us or the room we create in interaction to develop, present, and validate our self-concepts.

It will be the purpose of this chapter (1) to explore the nature, function, and scope of individual self-concepts, (2) to indicate the role self-concept plays in the interpersonal communication process, and (3) to examine the cueing, listening, and negotiating skills which undergird our capacity to create and sustain our visions of self.

The Nature, Function and Scope of Individual Self-Concepts

Approaching the study of interpersonal communication from a symbolic interactionist perspective, we find a long theoretical heritage which focuses upon the concepts of human action, self-concept, and symbolic interaction. Taylor (1968:33) incisively distinguishes human action from other types of behavior when he notes that to ascribe *action* to a person implies that: (1) a certain state of affairs came into existence, (2) the person intended this state of affairs (or something very close to it), and (3) the person's behaviors were, at least in part, instrumental in bringing the state of affairs into existence. Any explanation of human action requires an understanding of the actor's view of his relationship to those objects which he deems relevant to the action. We need a map of the environment as it appears to the actor. This map will not correspond to any "objective" description of the environment since it will exclude much and add more. The map will have to tell us what objects the individual will take into account and how, i.e., what his current conceptions are of his relations to relevant objects. It may be important to determine the degree to which the map is subject to alteration by the individual through a consideration of new objects or new properties of objects. In other words, we need some way of knowing the probable direction and content of changes in the map due to experience and, in particular, due to inputs of appropriately designed communication.

Following in the tradition of James, Cooley, and Mead, we shall argue that the self-concept is the generative mechanism for interpersonal choice and that an appropriate analysis of its contents and the processes it involves will provide us such a cognitive map. In the words of Blumer (1966:535), "The possession of a self provides the human being with a mechanism of self-interaction with which to meet the world . . . a mechanism that is used in forming and guiding his conduct." For Mead, the "self" meant that the human being is an object to its self. Blumer (1966:536) says, "With the mechanism of self-interaction the human being ceases to be a responding organism whose behavior is a product of what plays upon him from the outside, the inside, or both. Instead, he acts towards his world, interpreting what confronts him and organizing his actions on the basis of the interpretations."

Traditionally, the self-concept is viewed as the information an individual has regarding the relationship of objects or groups of objects to that person (Mead 1934). However, communication theorists need to subdivide the information an individual has regarding his relationship to objects based upon the quality of that information. We shall use the term *real self-concept* to refer to those self-object relationships which have been tested and supported in interaction. We shall use the term *ideal self-concept* to refer to those self-object relationships which an individual thinks exists, but which have either *not been* tested in interaction or *have been tested but not sustained* in interaction. The term *self-concept* will refer to both of those types of information. Mead's reason for positing such a conceptualization of self was that individuals, moving in their environment, are confronted by other persons, places, things, and messages. Individuals, when confronted by such objects, must, if they are to commit themselves to any action, perform two tasks. *First*, they must determine what the objects in their experience *are* by associating them with and differentiating them from other objects of their experience (i.e. these are friendly dogs). *Second*, they must determine the relationship of the objects to themselves in terms of appropriate actions in appropriate circumstances (i.e. I always pet friendly dogs). An individual's knowledge of what objects *are* and how one *should act* towards them is a product of information based on past experience. This does not mean an individual has in his experiential field only object relationships that include the self as one of the objects. The statement, "Aristotle is dead," for example, provides information about Aristotle without conveying anything about oneself. On the other hand, statements such as, "I am tall," "I am a good Democrat," and "I am a good teacher and therefore must have my papers graded on time," do provide information about oneself and would be a part of the self-concept.

Following Thompson (1972), self-object relationships can be divided into three classes. First, statements such as, "I am tall," designate relationships pertaining to what an individual is. They name or label an individual's attributes. These statements comprise the *identity self*. *Identity self-object relationships* tend to be *factual* (non-evaluative) *descriptions of one* in terms of physical characteristics, age, name, sex, place of residence, marriage, family, national or ethic background, social class, social role or position, church, job, group or organizational membership, and political party. Basically these statements are the type that appear on completed college entrance applications or job resumes. This information about you is typically public. A *second* class of self-object relationships reflects a person's feelings toward (or an *evaluation* of) those objects, such as "I am a *good* Democrat" or "I dislike hot foods." These statements form an individual's *evaluative self.* An *evaluative* self-object relationship reflects a *qualification or comment* on a factual description or an expression of feeling such as "I am sick, basically happy, good, too young, overly religious, good looking, sexy, stupid, glad to be here, happy with my job, and nice to be with." Finally, statements that, in addition to providing information for identifying and evaluating the self, prescribe an appropriate behavior to be performed in regard to the self-object relationship constitute the *behavioral self.* "I am a good teacher and therefore must have my papers graded on time," is an example of a behavioral self statement. *Behavioral self-object relationships* reflect *things one has done* (travel, hike, camp, fish, golf, play baseball, watch TV, buy records) or intends to do (go home, go to join a new organization, intend to change as a person, hope to ski or swim this weekend, want to buy a new album). Some statements may serve more than one category. The statement, "I am a good teacher who returns graded papers immediately," in addition to providing information for identifying and evaluating the self, prescribes an appropriate behavior for being a good teacher. Such statements carry two or three identifying markers.

The relationships that comprise the self-concept are important in at least three ways. First, the information an individual garners as a result of an encounter with one object will apply to all other objects one places in the same *class.* Thus, an individual can make inferences about his or her relationship to an object without encountering the object. One need only to have encountered another object that has been placed in the same category as the first.

Second, the self-concept provides us with *expectations* about the nature of objects placed in the same category (I.e., the self-concept directs perception). It causes people to take note of certain characteristics and to react to an object on the basis of those characteristics.

Third, as the self-concept develops, it provides us with *preconceived plans* of action. A self-object relationship constitutes a ready-made format for processing experience and initiating action. With such a system a person is prepared to cope with the future and to make sense out of the past.

Hence, the self-concept can be regarded as an organized set of information that defines the relationship of objects to the individual and is capable of governing and directing human action. Furthermore, the self-concept, as an organized set of structures, provides the rationale for choice in the form of a balanced repertory of alternative meanings, evaluations, and plans of action. Consequently, identity, evaluative, and behavioral self-object relations function as rules or imperatives for defining the self, evaluating objects or acting in specific situations where those objects are present.

The self-concept or rules which govern and guide an individual's relationship to objects by directing human perception, evaluations, and actions can always be stated such that in circumstance X, some perception, evaluation, or act is appropriate (Gottlieb 1968). Self-concept statements, formulated as rules, always contain:

(1) A definition of an object in terms of its relationship to the individual; e.g., I am the kind of person who attempts to be logical.

(2) An indication of the circumstances in which the rule is applicable; e.g., when dealing with others.

The composite of all the rules one has regarding the relationship of objects to one's self is one's self-concept. It is the stability of this set of rules that makes an individual's identity, evaluations, and behaviors predictable by others.

Central to our conceptualization of self-concept as the information one has regarding one's relationship to objects are five distinctions: (1) ideal-self, (2) real-self, (3) identity-self, (4) evaluative-self and (5) behavioral-self. A working knowledge of these types of self-concept rules can be obtained by filling out for any individual several *Twenty Question Statement Tests* (Kuhn and McPartland 1954). The Twenty Question Statement Test was designed as a simple test to elicit the underlying self-concept categories. For the purpose of illustration we shall provide one example of its use (you may want to perform such a test on yourself): First, a focal individual (in this case Don) is asked to complete the phrases, "I am—I like—I have done—," with twenty short (two or three word) statements. Second, two or more others with whom Don interacts are asked to fill out the same test on Don. Finally, these tests are then analyzed together. One begins the analysis by labeling all statements as identity, evaluative and/or behavioral self-concept categories. Next, one notes that some of those types of categories appear on all three lists, some on two and some on only one list. Those which appear on *all* lists are representations of his real-self. Those which appear on his list and only one other are representations of Don to himself and to that other person. Those are usually self-concept relationships in transition, and we will say more about them in the next chapter.

According to our Twenty Question Statement Test Dons' *real-self* (the self he can sustain in interaction with Lee and his mother) includes being intelligent, thoughtful, and a professor; likes teaching, traveling, and good food; dislikes chicken, and has written a book and traveled. Dons' *ideal-self* (the self he wants to be but which he has not effectively communicated to Lee or his mother) includes being aggressive, helpful; liking research; disliking rock music; having won five teaching awards.

Dons' *identity self-concept* consists of being *intelligent*, aggressive, *thoughtful*, helpful and a *professor* with the three underlined categories being stable (real-self) and predictive of his identity by others. Dons' *evaluative self-concept* consists of liking *teaching*, researching, *traveling*, *good food*, arguing, and disliking *chicken* and rock music, with the five underlined categories being stable (real-self) and a predictive of his evaluations by others. Dons' *behavioral self-concept* consists of

Table 2
Who then is Don?
(Twenty Question Statement Test on Don Cushman)

Don on Don			Don...	Lee on Don	Don's mother on Don
1. I am intelligent.	I	Real	is	intelligent	my son
2. I am aggressive.	I	Ideal	is	hard working	a professor
3. I am thoughtful.	I	Real	is	helpful	an excellent teacher
4. I am helpful.	I	Ideal	is	thoughtful	intelligent
5. I am a Professor.	I	Real	is	a professor	thoughtful
6. I like teaching.	E	Real	likes	to travel	to travel
7. I like researching.	E	Ideal	likes	good food	good food
8. I like traveling.	E	Real	likes	to argue	to argue
9. I like good food.	E	Real	likes	dancing	his father
10. I like to argue.	E	Real	likes	teaching	his work
11. I dislike chicken.	E	Real	dislikes	chicken	chicken
12. I dislike rock music.	E	Ideal	dislikes	lazy people	coming home
13. I have written a book.	B	Real	has	written a book	traveled a lot
14. I have traveled to Korea.	B	Real	has	gone to Korea	won many awards
15. I have won five teaching awards.	B	Ideal	has	gone to Australia	written a book
etc.				etc.	etc.

—————————underline–real-self

having *written a book, traveled to Korea* and won five teaching awards, with the underlined concepts being stable (real-self) and predictive of his behavior by others.

Who are you? You may want to repeat this exercise to see who you are to yourself and others.

The Role Self-Concept Plays in Interpersonal Communication Processes

It should be evident by now that we regard the self-concept as the composite of identity, evaluation, and behavioral rules regarding one's real and ideal relationship to objects, and that the stability of those rules is predictive of our actions. We do not, however, suggest that the process by which a person forms and executes his or her actions is completely determined prior to an act's being undertaken. An action, Mead asserts, encompasses a complete span of intention from its initial impulse through its termination, in our evaluation of its execution from both our point of view and the point of view of others. Between initiation and termination the individual may construct, organize, and reorganize a plan of action based on feedback. Two distinct types of feedback are recognizable: *positive* and *negative* feedback.

Negative feedback works to correct an individual's behavior when that behavior strays from the desired goal. Negative feedback provides information to an individual about that individual's progress towards some goal. This information is used to adjust the individual's performance. *The self-concept provides the individual with both his or her information about goals and the rules for how to adjust the individual's performance so as to obtain the goals.* Positive feedback is dependent upon an individual's obtaining information about new ways of organizing action. It allows a very small, almost random push in an improbable direction to be recognized as beneficial and then to orient the individual's old course of action to a new course which maximizes those benefits. The judgment that a new course of action is beneficial and worth pursuing requires a previous organizational pattern for comparison purposes. The self-concept provides the previous pattern of organization and the information needed to recognize the implications of the new pattern.

Positive and negative feedback provide a dynamic quality to the self-concept and allow for its development and adaptation in particular situations. However, in most instances of human action, the evidence in favor of one self-concept rule over another is so overwhelming that the action takes place instantly. Many situations are of a sufficently recurrent nature and the self-object relations come to mind so quickly that they seem to happen automatically.

Since the self-concept serves as a coordinator of positive and negative feedback in developing and adjusting our self-object relationships in specific situations, we would expect scientific research to indicate both a substantial and a necessary relationship between an individual's self-concepts and his or her ability to comprehend messages from others, construct messages adapted to others, and influence the behavior of others.

A careful review of empirical research reveals just such a relationship. *First,* over ten scientific studies reveal that the number of self-object relationships, or the *scope* and the amount of information one has about each self-object relationship, or the depth of self-concept, explain between 16% and 54% of our capacity to understand messages from others (Cushman, Valentinsen and Dietrich 1982:101). *Second,* some six scientific studies indicate that the degree of differentiation of self-object relationships or scope, and the level of self-object relationship or abstractness of self-concept explain between 16% and 54% of our ability to adapt messages to others, self-concepts (Burleson 1980). *Finally,* several scientific studies reveal a substantial and necessary relationship between *self-concept strength* and one's ability to overcome one's own anxiety, control the behavior of others and reach a consensus with them (Cushman, Valentinsen and Dietrich 1982:101-3).

What then can we conclude from our rather brief survey of the scientific research? It seems safe to conclude that an individual's self-concept (the information one has regarding one's relationship to objects) can be seen to occupy a significant and necessary position in regulating an individual's communicative effectiveness in human interaction.

Listening, Cueing, and Negotiating Skills

An individual can only construct and sustain his or her self-concept in interaction with another. Only in communication can individuals define and interpret objects and their relationship to self and test the consensus of others regarding that relationship.*Listening* skills determine one's ability to identify different types of statements and the self-object relationships designated by them. By improved listening, one enhances one's ability to take the role of another and more accurately develop expectations for one's self. *Cueing skills* reflect one's ability to translate one's relationship to objects for the understanding by diverse others. By improved cueing, one enhances one's ability to provide someone else with the information necessary to develop clear expectations toward one's actions. *Negotiating skills* improve one's ability to recognize the positions of others, to state one's own position, and to develop appropriate means for reconciling differences in one's own and others' expectations. By improving one's negotiating skills, one improves substantially the probability of sustaining one's self-concept among diverse others.

Listening and cueing skills. Understanding others and getting them to understand us are the most fundamental problems of human interaction. These problems can be made more difficult by language and background differences, inattention, or unclear thinking. While these general constraints will always influence the effectiveness of communication, several specific constraints emerge which accentuate the problem of understanding based on our specific analysis of the interpersonal communication process. Let us begin by exploring several of these specific constraints.

If our primary interest in interpersonal communication is the relationship of objects to individuals and understanding clearly and accurately what we and others propose these relationships to be, then several specific listening and cueing problems emerge. *First,* when someone talks, we must be very clear about the type of information they are providing. Since it is sometimes difficult for people to recognize the various types of information they can have about themselves and others, we propose the following categories as suggestive for alerting us to (or sharpening our awareness of) different types of statements.

> *thoughts* — perceptions, attitudes, interpretations, ideas, beliefs, expectations, stereotypes, assumptions.
> *feelings* — emotions such as anger, joy, sorrow.
> *intentions* — wants, goals, desires, assertions, denials.
> *actions* — role behaviors, inactions including silence.[2]

Second, whenever others make one of these type of statements, it is of the utmost importance that we determine whether they are asserting or denying (1) *their* relationship to an object, (2) other's relationship to an object, (3) a characteristic of the object, or (4) a report on someone else's perception of our's and others' relationship to an object. *For example,* when someone says Don is ill, it is uncertain without further cueing whether this is a report by someone of what was heard, an assertion of an observation of Don, or Don's characterization of himself. Is it an instance of an identify, or an evaluative or behavioral self-object relationship? Only proper cueing or questioning by a careful listener can clarify the meaning of such statements. *Third,* when confronted by such statements a careful listener has at least two strategies for clarifying his understanding of such statements. Careful listeners *check out* other's statements in order to assist in self-concept presentation. Here the listener specifies what he or she is observing in the communicator's messages, or asks for clarifying information.

What do you think about—?
How do you feel about—?
What do you intend to do about—?
What are you doing about—?

Careful listeners also perform *reflective listening* by feeding back to the communicator what they heard or observed.

I hear you saying that you think—.
I'm hearing that you intend to do—.
You are saying that you feel—.
I think you're doing—.

Effective listening skills enable the listener to avoid erroneous assumptions and thereby enhance accurate perception of the other's self-concept. Careful listeners make sure that the *proper referent* for statements of self-object relationship are present.

Did Don say that?
Is that your observation?
Where did you hear that?
On what is that statement based?

Negotiating skills. In a world marked by cultural, group, and individual diversity and interdependence, it is quite common for two or more people to have divergent and sometimes competing views regarding an individual's relationship to objects or one's self-concept. Conflict in such a situation may be viewed as a condition in which the concerns of two or more parties appear incompatible. When that happens, one is in need of a framework and procedures for dealing constructively with those differences. Thomas (1977) provides a two-dimensional analysis of various conflict resolution procedures based upon the communicator's underlying intent. *Assertiveness*, or the intent to satisfy one's own interests, is the first dimension, while *cooperativeness*, or the intent to help others satisfy their interests, is the second dimension. Five negotiating approaches emerge from such an analysis.

Within the literature on conflict resolution the most commonly employed negotiating strategies are the *competitive* (I win, you lose), *compromise* (I get half, you get half) and *collaboration* (I get what I want and you get what you want) outcomes.

> *Competition* is an attempt to arrive at a win-lose solution which favors oneself. Competitive behaviors involve the use of power to force the other party into submission on a given issue.
>
> *Compromise* is an attempt to seek an acceptable solution of gains and losses for both parties. In contrast to collaborative outcomes which maximally satisfy both parties, compromise outcomes leave the concerns of each party partially dissatisfied and partially satisfied. Behaviorally, compromise involves an exchange of offers and the negotiation of trade-offs or concessions.
>
> *Collaboration* is an attempt to find integrative outcomes that satisfy both parties. Behaviorally, it involves confronting the differences, sharing information about both parties' concerns, and problem-solving to find an integrative solution that satisfies both sets of concerns.
>
> (Thomas 1972:52-58)

In interpersonal communication one presents one's vision of self to those intimate others from whom one seeks and needs support in order to sustain one's view of self. *Competitive* bargaining leads to the domination of one individual's interests over those of another. Such a negotiating procedure would over time lead to a withdrawal of support by one side from interaction and to a failure of self-concept verification. *Compromise* bargaining may on occasion be useful, but it is hard to form a compromise, to see that "you get half and I get half" when we see different issues as important and want different outcomes. *Collaborative* bargaining appears to be an ideal interpersonal conflict resolution procedure because as Derr (1978) argues:

1. Open and honest interaction promotes authentic interpersonal relations.
2. Conflict is used as a creative force for innovation and improvement.
3. Process of collaboration enhances feedback and information flow.
4. Solving of disputes increases feelings of integrity, trusting in climate.

Collaborative bargaining can thus be seen as a mode of interpersonal conflict resolution aimed at developing an integrated consensus through argumentation and role-taking. When successfully utilized, it results not only in the cessation of conflict but in modifying the cognitive framework of the individuals involved to a consensus framework which respects individual differences.

Table 3

A Two-Dimensional Model of Conflict Intentions

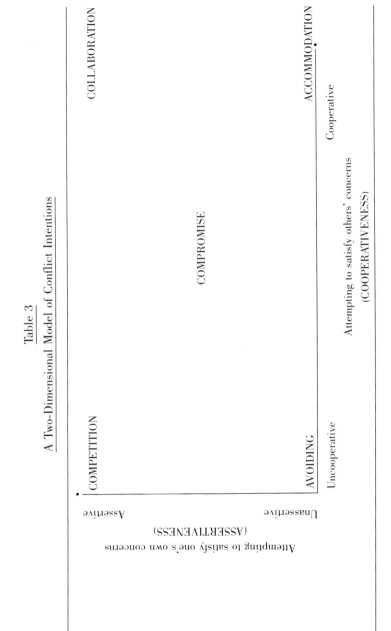

COMPETITION

COLLABORATION

COMPROMISE

AVOIDING

ACCOMMODATION

Assertive

Unassertive

(ASSERTIVENESS)
Attempting to satisfy one's own concerns

Uncooperative

Cooperative

Attempting to satisfy others' concerns
(COOPERATIVENESS)

Source: Adapted from Kenneth W. Thomas, "Conflict and Conflict Management," in Marvin D. Dunnett, ed., *Handbook of Industrial and Organizational Psychology* (Chicago: Rand-McNally, 1976), p. 900.

Eiseman (1978) outlines the steps involved in collaborative bargaining:

1. Identifying recurring patterns of interaction;
2. Establishing each party's theories-in-use, i.e., the desires and beliefs which direct the party's behavior;
3. Constructing an integrative conceptual framework which (a) builds upon the theories-in-use of each party, (b) demonstrates that everyone's desires are compatible, and (c) provides a way of thinking about the conflict which all parties can support;
4. Helping the parties explore (a) the nature and implications of the integrative conceptual framework, (b) the steps and costs involved in acquiring the new patterns of interaction implied, and (c) any reservations existing about abandoning both the old patterns and the beliefs which support them;
5. Helping the parties clarify whatever concepts support the new patterns and build whatever skills are needed to enact them; and
6. Helping the parties undergo the transition from the old to the new, stabilize the new patterns, and assume the full responsibility for maintaining them.

The central problem of negotiation in collaborative bargaining is step three, the construction of a collaborative solution. In collaborative bargaining a conflict is only considered resolved when each party is convinced the final solution satisfactorily embodies all the party's initial positions. Eiseman outlines six principles for formulating such a solution:

Principle 1: Dimensionalize the perceptions. Here we may contrast the "Aristotelian" and "Galileian" modes of thought: Aristotle utilizes categorical concepts, whereas Galileo employs dimensional concepts. When one proceeds from the former to the latter one is able to treat every concept as variable in nature rather than essential. Thus, the perception of practical problems and relationships can be treated as involving variable contents, no one of which is absolutely essential.

Principle 2: Increase the dimensionality of each participant's analysis of both the problem and the relationships involved. Most times if one increases the dimensionality of the framework containing each of the participant's views by one, at least one new principle for coordinating action or reordering perceptions within the conceptual framework will emerge.

Principle 3: Search for orthogonal dimensions. Introducing an orthogonal dimension involves reordering the participants' views of a problem from a flanking perspective. Such a reordering creates an entirely new perspective from which to view all the perceptions in the old framework.

Principle 4: Construct ideal principles for solving the problem. If each party to a conflict can create such an ideal type, then collectively they may provide clues as to the common elements of a solution across perspectives.

Principle 5: Explore possible semantic solutions to the problem. This involves teasing out the dimensions of key words so as to include or exclude underlying dimensions.

Principle 6: Construct composite variables. If a conflict cannot be resolved semantically, then it must be resolved propositionally by combining variables perceived as necessary to a satisfactory solution to a problem.

The use of these six principles should, according to Cushman and Tompkins (1980), lead to one of four types of outcomes. *First,* one may generate *an identity solution.* This happens when, through open and frank discussion, two parties discover that what were seemingly divergent view-points are in fact common perceptions of a problem and the use of common values in selecting among alternative solutions. For example: you assert that you are beautiful, while I assert that in fact you are only attractive. We discuss the issue and find that while we do have semantic differences in word choice our characterizations of the attributes of both attractive and beautiful are similar. *Second,* one may generate *an integrative solution.* This happens when the individual who needs to resolve a problem sees the problem the same way but employs diverse values in selecting from among solutions. For example, you assert that you are forceful and fair, but I feel that one who is forceful cannot also be fair. However, we conclude that one can be firm and equitable. Our solution integrates qualities of both initial positions into a mutually satisfactory solution. *Third,* one may generate *a value solution.* When the individuals needing to resolve a problem have similar values but do not see the same problem, their common values may lead one to help the other. For example, I like Sue because she is thoughtful, and you like Jane for the same reason. You want to send Jane flowers because she is thoughtful, but have no money. So, because of our common values, I will lend you the money to buy Jane flowers. *Fourth,* one may generate a *stand-off solution.* When the individuals needing to resolve some conflict neither see the same problem nor hold common values, they may choose to do nothing.

Our own interpersonal communicative competence determines the range and types of self-object relationships we can create and sustain in human interaction with diverse, yet interdependent, others. Our listening, cueing, and negotiating skills place limits upon our interpersonal communication competence.

In conclusion, the self-concept is a communication-specific construct. It is formed and sustained in human interaction. It is basic to coordination which is accomplished only by communication. Thus, the self-concept becomes a necessary and sufficient element that coordinates and initiates positive and negative feedback in adjusting human perception and behavior to concrete situations.

Propositions

1. The self-concept is the information an individual has regarding his relationships to objects.

2. Our real-self concept consists of all those self-object relationships that have been presented and sustained in interaction.

3. Our *ideal-self* concept consists of all those self-object relationships which have either not been presented or not been sustained in interaction.

4. Our self-concept consists of identity, evaluative, and behavioral self-object relationships.

5. Our self-concept allows us to make inferences, hold expectations, and formulate plans for action based on the similarity of objects to previous self-object relationships.

6. The stability of our self-concept is what makes our identity, evaluations, and behaviors predictable by others.

7. The self-concept provides individuals with both information about goals and the rules for how to adjust their performance to obtain the goals so that they may adapt as a result of positive and negative feedback.

8. The self-concept scientifically has a strong and necessary effect upon message comprehension, message adaptation, and our ability to overcome anxiety, control others' behaviors, and reach a consensus.

9. An individual's ability to construct and sustain his or her self-concept in interaction is dependent upon listening, cueing, and negotiating skills.

Notes

1. Portions of this chapter were previously published in D. Cushman, B. Valentinsen, and D. Dietrich, "A Rules Theory of Interpersonal Relationship", in *Comparative Theories of Human Communication*, (ed. F.X. Dance, New York, NY: Harper Row, 1982), 90–107.

2. Adapted from S. Miller, E. Nunnally, and D. Wackman, *Alive and Aware*, 30–31. Minneapolis, Minn: Interpersonal Communication Programs, Inc., 1975.

References

Blumer, H. Commentary and Debate. *American Journal of Sociology* 71:535–45, 1966.

Burleson, B.R. *Development and Individual Differences in Comfort Intended Message Strategies: Four Empirical Studies.* Diss. University of Illinois, 1980.

Cahn, D.D. Interpersonal Communication and Transactional Relationships: Clarification and Application. *Communication Quarterly* 24:38–44, 1976.

Cushman, D., and Tompkins, P.K. A Theory of Rhetoric for Contemporary Society. *Philosophy and Rhetoric.* 13:43-67, 1980.

Cushman, D., Valentinsen, B., and Dietrich, D. A Rules Theory of Interpersonal Relationships. In *Comparative Theories of Human Communication*, ed. F.X. Dance, 90–107. New York, NY: Harper Row, 1982.

Derr, C.B. Managing Organizational Conflict. *California Management Review.* 21:78–79, 1978.

Eiseman, J.W. Reconciling Incompatible Positions. *Journal of Applied Behavioral Science.* 14:132–140, 1978.

Gottlieb, C. *The Logic of Choice*, New York, NY: Macmillan, 1968.

Haller, A.O. The Wisconsin Significant Other Battery. *Final Research Report U.S. Office of Education Grant 351170.* Washington D.C.: U.S. Dept. of Health, Education, and Welfare, 1970.

Kuhn, M.H., and McPartland, T. An Empirical Investigation of Self-Attitudes. *American Sociological Review.* 19:68–76, 1954.

Mead, G. H. *Mind, Self, and Society.* Chicago, IL: University of Chicago Press, 1934.

Taylor, C. *The Explanation of Behavior*, New York, NY: Humanities Press, 1968.

Thomas, K.W. "Introduction." *California Management Review.* 21:56–60, Winter 1978.

Thomas, K. W. Toward Multi-Dimensional Value in Teaching: The Example of Conflict Behavior. *Academy of Management Review.* 2:448, 1977.

Thompson, W. *Correlates of the Self-Concept: Studies on Self-Concept and Rehabilitation.* Nashville, TN: Nashville Counselor Recording Tests, 1972.

3

Interpersonal Communication and the Development, Presentation, and Validation of Individual Self-Concepts

> *Interpersonal communication* has as it principal goal the co-ordination of human activity in regard to the *development, presentation*, and *validation* of *individual self-concepts*. If an individual's self-concept is viewed as the information he has regarding his relationship to objects, then the development, presentation, and validation of an individual's self-concept will take the form of descriptions, assertions, and denials regarding an individual's relationship to objects and others.
>
> D. Cushman and T. Florence (1974:12-13).

Self-Concept Support and Denial: The Focus of Interpersonal Interaction

One coordinated task amid the many recurrent tasks within a culture is based on the premise that each individual, if that individual is to undertake an action, must determine who he is and how he relates, or wants to relate, to objects and others in his environment. Through communication, individuals describe and propose their preferred relationship to objects or others; e.g. I love you, I dislike hamburger, I am going bald, I want to be your friend, and I am fat. These descriptions and assertions are questioned and then accepted or rejected by others using communication. In this manner, individuals learn who they are and how they can and cannot relate to others. Only then can an individual develop intentions regarding his preferred relationships to objects and others and the means for actualizing them.

Manifesting support for, or denying, another's self-concept is contingent upon a recognition of the unique scope, depth, and configuration of that other's self-concept and upon one's knowledge and skill in the use of communication to create messages and convey such support or denial. Five dimensions appear significant for the creation of messages that convey self-concept support or denial. We may focus on an individual's identity, evaluative, or behavioral self-object relationships, and we may address an individual's ideal- or real-self. Messages that seek to manipulate self-concept support or denial must employ one or more of these dimensions in providing self-concept support or denial. The processes of giving and obtaining such information are central to the development, presentation, and validation of individual self-concepts or interpersonal communication. The remainder of this chapter will explore the communication processes involved in (1) the development of individual self-concepts, (2) the presentation of them, and (3) the validation of individual self-concepts.

Self-Concept Development

If the basic determinant of differential human behavior is an individual's information regarding his relationship to objects, then it becomes apparent that all the ways in which an individual can become aware of those relationships are the ways in which the self-concept is formed and develops. Mead argued that the process of self-concept development is basically a process of socialization or acculturation. The individual is born into ongoing cultural and social institutions which provide him with an initial repertory of potential self-object relationships. Then, through the social learning process an individual is made aware of sets of rules regarding his relationship to those objects or others. Family and work patterns as well as language and interactional patterns are passed on in such a manner.

According to Mead (1934:327) *role-taking* is the central mechanism for the development of a self-concept and for understanding the self-concepts of others. The term "role" is defined as a socially prescribed way of behaving in particular situations for any person occupying a given cultural or social organizational position. A role represents what a person is supposed to do in a given situation by virtue of the position he holds. Role-taking is the process whereby an individual imaginatively constructs the attitudes and expectations others have for him when he assumes a given role. This allows him to predict others' behavior toward him when he occupies the role (Mead 1934:243). Through the role-taking process, a process which exhibits a developmental history, an individual is made aware of an increasing range of self-object relationships.

Building on the work of Turner (1956) and Lauer and Boardman (1971), we shall differentiate four levels of role-taking. *Basic role-taking* is the process whereby an individual imaginatively constructs the attitudes and expectations of cultural and social organizational positions and is consequently able to anticipate and respond to the roles of others. Basic role-taking involves understanding what it means to be a father, a mother, a policeman, an American, a gas station attendant and other standardized cultural and organizational roles. Common basic roles in our culture are son, daughter, godfather, godmother, businessman, politician, lawyer, cook, waitress, mailman, salesman, auto mechanic, repairman, teller, student, administrator, clerk, usher, priest, and others. *Reflective role-taking* is the evaluation of various role requirements in regard to an individual's likes and dislikes. Two types of information are required for such a comparison: information regarding the cultural and social organizational role acquired through basic role-taking and information about an individual's self-concept, his likes and dislikes. As a teacher, I like giving lectures and dislike grading papers; as a father I like being head of the house and I dislike giving my children money; as an American, I like being patriotic and I dislike paying taxes. *Common reflective* role-taking characteristics in our culture are, I like this, don't like that, this is good, this is bad, do this, don't do that, good-looking, ugly, satisfied with this, dissatisfied with that, happy, sad, and so forth. *Appropriative role-taking* entails an individual's evaluation of some aspect of a role positively and the reduction of that self-object relationship to a permanent part of the personality or self-concept. It leads to the acquisition of a self-concept rule. For example, a male high school student might be a debater and find that he likes one aspect of the role, namely, the aggressive testing of arguments. He may then make that aspect of the role a permanent part of his personality. This means that even when he leaves the role of debater he will take the opportunity to exercise that aspect of his personality whenever possible. Through appropriative role-taking a person develops a set of self-object relations which are person-dependent rather than role-dependent. Those relations are the set of characteristics one manifests across roles, or one's self-concept. For example, one has to appropriate such self-concept relationships as pushy, arrogant, or forceful. One has to decide to be that way. *Common appropriative* role-taking characteristics in our culture are active, classy, demanding, emotional, honest, assertive, moody, religious, satisfied, talkative, temperamental, creative, dreamy, excitable, humble, lazy, interesting, practical, intelligent, perfectionist, protective, rude, sociable, romantic, stupid, and so on. *Synesic role-taking* is the imaginative construction of the other's self-concept such that one can separate another's *basic and reflective* self-object relationship from one's appropriative and synesic, and can address one's appropriative and synesic self-object relationships. In so doing, others will note your ability to respond positively to others' intimate self and will characterize you as thoughtful, caring, and empathic. These are characteristics you can only have by taking another point of view and supporting their unique self-object relationships. Common synesic- role-taking characteristics in our culture are cooperative, understanding, sympathetic, adaptive, consensual, kind, loving, friendly, helpful, patient, sensitive, other-oriented, and tolerant.

The stratification of role-taking by awareness levels has several important implications. *First, basic, reflective, appropriative, and synesic* role-taking represent progressively greater orders of interpersonal awareness. Interpersonal awareness enables individuals to comprehend the expectations of others. *Basic* and *reflective* role-taking are processes one employs to learn and evaluate previously established roles and their expectations. These two levels of role-taking presuppose the existence of mechanisms other than the self-concept to generate such roles. Basic and reflective role-taking are thus restricted to the cultural and organizational systems of communication. Appropriative and synesic role-taking are processes one employs to develop, present, and validate individual self-concepts. These two levels of role-taking presuppose the existence of the self-concept as the mechanism generating behavior. Appropriative and synesic role-taking are thus restricted to the interpersonal level of communication systems.

Second, self-concept development takes place throughout one's life. One is continually being placed in new cultural and organizational roles, evaluating these roles, appropriating aspects of a role to oneself, and recognizing the growth in others in a similar manner. This continual growth increases the scope, depth, and configuration of individual self-concepts. The failure to grow at a reasonable rate leads the members of society to characterize one as immature. A rapid rate of growth leads to a characterization of maturity.

Third, the development of your self-concept, and the scope, depth, and configuration of your self-object relationships constrain the number and type of others who can and will provide self-concept support or denial for you. This constraint in turn limits the kinds and number of people who can or will want to be your friends, lovers, and mates.

Fourth, the rate of change in your self-concept development is an important predictor of how long your relationship with others will last. If one changes faster than another, a strain is placed on the relationship. If both change together in similar or supportable directions, the relationship grows. If both change in unsupportable directions the relationship terminates.

Central to an understanding of the four implications is some familiarity with the issues involved in self-concept development, support, denial, and change. A working knowledge of these issues can again be developed through the use of the Twenty Questions Statement Test of a focal individual and that person's family and friends. Allow us to illustrate our point through an example. Below are listed the real-self concept characteristics of Lee, Don, and Bill. Those characteristics were generated by having each member of the family do a Twenty Questions Statement Test on themselves and each other. Then by a cross-person comparision the following real self-concepts emerged. These characteristics will first be labeled as *Basic, Reflective, Appropriative,* and *Synesic* for each and then alone and in combination with others.

According to our Twenty Statement Test, Lee, Don, and Bill have fairly evenly developed self-concepts in that they contain several basic, reflective, appropriative, and synesic self-concept characteristics, evenly distributed between the cultural and organizational or basic and reflective levels and the interpersonal or appropriative and synesic levels. An even distribution is preferable because, if one level dominates, certain specific types of problem emerge when one interacts with other people. *If one's self-concept consists primarily of basic roles,* then there is only a cultural, organizational self present. There is no unique interpersonal self with whom others can form an interpersonal relationship. One will always be treated as a role (as only a father or mother) rather than also as a friend. One will also be poor at recognizing and responding to another's interpersonal self. *If one's self-concept consists primarily of reflective characteristics,* one is only evaluative. There is no basic and appropriative self to guide positive actions, nor a synesic self to support others. Positive self-concept support is tied to common evaluations between others. *If one's self-concept consists primarily of appropriative characteristics,* then one always acts as one wants irrespective of what others want; one lacks an appreciation of who others are and tends to use others as objects. Such a person responds to the basic roles and reflective qualities of others by not recognizing

Table 4

Real Self-concepts for Lee, Don, and Bill

by Role-taking Levels

Lee real-self		Don real-self		Bill real-self	
1. Professor	B	Intelligent	A	Professor	B
2. Married	A	Assertive	A	Researcher	B
3. Teacher	B	Talkative	A	Status Conscious	A
4. Researcher	B	Helpful	S	Meek	A
5. Likes good food	R	Thoughtful	S	Insecure	A
6. Likes travel	R	Professor	B	Dislikes criticism	R
7. Assertive	A	Teacher	B	Intelligent	A
8. Helpful	S	Researcher	B	Dislikes conflict	R
9. Talkative	A	Likes travel	R	Concerned	S
10. Thoughtful	S	Likes good food	R	Friendly	S

A = Appropriate
B = Basic
R = Reflective
S = Synesic

them and by asserting only an interpersonal self. *If one's self-concept consists primarily of synesic characteristics*, then one is only doing what others want. One has no basic or appropriative self to guide positive actions and no evaluative or reflective self to distinguish good from bad. One is whoever others want one to be.

Moreover, according to Lee's and Don's twenty question statement tests both have similar roles (professor, teacher, researcher), reflective (likes good food, likes to travel), appropriative (talkative, assertive) and synesic (helpful, thoughtful) self-concept qualities at this time. They may or may not have arrived at this point in the same manner, but at least for now their rate of self-concept development has considerable commonality. When we add Bill to this group there is some similarity (professor, researcher), but also a lot of diversity.

Furthermore, according to Lee and Don's Twenty Statement Tests they both have a similar scope, depth, and configuration of self-concept in the areas of professor and its underlying qualities of teacher and researcher and in the areas of liking good food and travel and in being assertive, talkative, and helpful. This common scope and depth indicates high positive self-concept support between them and little for them to disagree on that is fundamental to the self. As we shall see in the next chapter, this is a paradigm friendship relationship. In addition, the scope, depth, and configuration of self-concept characteristics are such that a large number of people in this culture could support those qualities. If they had been mean, thoughtless, and criminal that would not have been the case. Again when we add Bill to the group we have some similarities and many differences. Lee, Don, and Bill can provide positive self-concept support on professor, researcher, intelligent, concern and friendliness. But Lee's and Don's aggressive and talkative tendencies may threaten Bill who is meek, insecure, and status conscious. In addition, these same characteristics of Bill will not receive a good deal of support from other people in the culture in that they are culturally understandable.

Finally, it is hard to tell from the Twenty Statement Test whether Don and Lee will change rapidly in the near future, since we have no Twenty Statement Tests repeated over time. However, it does appear this will not happen. The reason for this is that they have so much in common now and that they hold real-self concepts indicating a high degree of stability. However, it is certain that Bill will change his self-concept in different directions from Lee and Don if he interacts frequently with them. They will, by their assertiveness, weaken Bill's view of himself as intelligent, and, perhaps, as a researcher, if he meets frequent criticism during their interactions.

It may be very useful for you to repeat this exercise on yourself and one or more friends. In so doing you should keep the following in mind.

Problems in interpersonal relationships may occur when people are at the same or different levels. For example, suppose two people are synesic. Without a dominant, assertive partner, they do not know what to feel, do, or want. Each is waiting to hear what the other wants. Or, suppose two persons are at the appropriative level and have compatible needs and feelings. They may have few sources of conflict, because of the level involved, but if they disagree on specifically what they want and need, a great deal of conflict may result. In this case, they compete against each other in a win-lose situation in which one may satisfy his or her needs at the expense of the other. Finally, suppose one person is at the synesic level and the other is at the appropriative level. The latter receives and gets self-concept validation, while the former does the giving and does not get self-concept validation.

Thus, by determining how people view themselves and others one can see if they clash or support each other by role-taking levels or on specific content regarding self-concepts. A synesic person may find compatibility with an appropriative partner, especially if on specific characteristics they think alike. They fit together relationally and individually; they are matched on content and relationships. In another case, two people may share values, but one wants to act on them (appropriative) while the other merely talks about them (reflective). They may fit together on content (they want and value the same things) but clash at the relational level.

In addition, by looking at the test results for oneself and others, one can determine how healthy the communication environment is. Suppose, for example, Fred lists on the test the following characteristics: uptight, oversensitive, weak self-concept, and blows up easily. Suppose further that Fred finds that all his friends have strong self-concepts, are dominant, aggressive, confident, and critical.

Poor Fred may feel like a featherweight in a boxing ring with heavyweights. He is tentative while the others are aggressive and probably critical of his lack of assertiveness. Such a network of interpersonal relationships is obviously self-defeating for Fred. Suppose, however, Fred is surrounded by synesic people. They would be so helpful that his insecurity and other characteristics would pose no problem for the relationships.

The development of an individual's self-concept can be very suggestive in regard to the kinds of people who will support and deny his relationship to objects and the kinds of cultural, organizational, and interpersonal relationships he or she can enter into with others. However, each of us has some control over who we are and which parts of our self-concepts are presented to which others for approval or denial. Attention in the remainder of this chapter will focus on these issues.

The Presentation of Individual Self-Concepts

If our self-concept is formed in interaction with others and our real-self consists of those self-object relationships that we present and sustain in interaction, then two very different tendencies exert pressure upon us when we consider when and before whom to present portions of our self-concept. *First,* if one's self-concept consists of the information regarding one's relationship to objects and if such relationships when validated enable one to predict and control their social environment, then we would assume that most people would be well motivated to insure that their self-conceptions are accurate and reliable. One way to do this is to attempt to acquire social feedback which represents a *strong test* of one's specific self-object relationship. *Second,* if one values a specific self-object relationship and has doubts either about that relationship or about one's ability to communicate that relationship, one may choose to provide a *weak* test of that relationship by presenting it only to preferred others who one knows will not challenge it, in order to preserve one's vision of self. In the face of these two very diverse tendencies several scholars have investigated how most people balance these diverse interests and the styles of communication involved in presenting one's self to others (Cushman and Craig 1976; Norton 1978). We can better understand the strategies involved in the presentation of self if we explore communicator style and its two underlying dimensions . . . risk and disclosure.

Risk refers to how a communicator limits others' responses to one's messages. A *low risk* statement is exemplifed by "I look very good in this dress, don't I?" In a low risk statement the communicator minimizes personal risk by selecting a specific self-object relationship and structuring the message sent about it in such a manner as to cue others as to how they should legitimately and coherently respond. A *high risk* statement is exemplifed by "How do you like this?" A high risk statement fails to prescribe an acceptable response and hence increases personal risk by allowing an unknown response. *Disclosure* is employed in the traditional sense of the term. *Low disclosure* is minimal exposure by a communicator of information regarding one unique (ideal) self-concept. A low disclosure statement is exemplifed by "I am a college student." While this statement does provide information about a communicator's self-concept, it provides little information that a person living in our culture and familar with the role of college student could not have inferred without having talked to one. A *high disclosure* statement occurs when one provides information to another which reveals information about one's self-concept that the other person could not arrive at, except by understanding one's interpersonal self. A high risk statement is exemplifed by "I have always hated men with big veins on their right front toe." Such information as this reflects not a cultural or organizational role-characteristic (a self-object relationship which anyone in the culture or organization is familar with) but an individual's unique self-object relationship.

If we apply our analysis of risk and disclosure to our previously developed topology of role-taking levels, we generate four communicative styles in self-concept presentation. *Basic role-takers* will generate messages which are *conventional* in that when one person in a cultural or organizational role communicates with another person in a cultural or organizational role; what he or she communicates is not individual-specific. Such information will be low on risk and low on disclosure in that how a person in one role is suppose to respond to a person in another role is tightly prescribed and in that such communications tell us little about the unique self of the people involved. *Reflective role-takers* will generate messages which are *interpersonal* in that they tell the listener what the sender personally likes or doesn't not like about a socially prescribed role. Interpersonal messages will be low on risk in that one is telling another of one's personal views of a role, which, such, is seldom challenged. Such messages are high in disclosure since they express how the unique self responds to the social role. *Appropriative role-takers* will generate messages which are *manipulative* in nature since they are attempting to get the listener to accept the senders' individually preferred self-object relationship. Such messages will be high in risk because the listener may not let the sender maintain a preferred relationship to an object, but low on disclosure in that until the sender does it you will know little about his or her unique self. Of course, afterwards you may know a great deal. *Synesic role-takers* will generate messages that are *open* in content, both high on risk and high on disclosure. When one reacts to another interpersonal self honestly and frankly, one is both high in risk and high in disclosure. To open oneself in this manner is to allow for the possibility of change.

As one can see from our Twenty Questions Statement Test analysis, most people have basic, reflective, appropriative, and synesic qualities as part of their self-concepts. Most people in turn may employ any one of these interaction styles they wish, depending on which aspects of their self-concepts they choose to present to others. Research on this topic reveals a rather common pattern in the use of these various communication styles. If one is interacting with the kind of person one dislikes, then that individual will usually employ a *conventional communication style in order to restrict communication to the highly predictable basic role level.* On the other hand, if one is contemplating marrying some other, one usually discloses his or her most intimate interpersonal self in a high risk situation, thus

Table 5

Communicator Style and Role-Taking Levels:

a Comparison

Role-Taking Levels	Communicator Style	Risk	Disclosure
1. Basic	Conventional	Low	Low
2. Reflective	Interpersonal	Low	High
3. Appropriative	Manipulative	High	Low
4. Synesic	Open	High	High

employing an open communication style in order to see how the other handles or interacts on such topics as a preliminary to setting up a permanent interpersonal relationship.

However, most of our interactions with others fall in between these extremes. Here again scientific research has discovered a very persistent pattern in our interactions (Swan and Read 1981). *In most situations people seek out positive self-concept support* for their self-concept, by presenting only those self-object relationships which they believe, based on past experience, specific others will support. The particular self-presentation strategy that one will employ depends upon whether one is *initiating*, in the *midst* of, or *reflecting* back on a given interaction. *First*, in initiating interaction aimed at testing a specific self-object relationship, one is more likely to search out others whom one believes will provide a positive appraisal. Even when a negative evaluation is presented by surprise, along with positive evaluations, we are more likely to attend to only the positive response. *Second*, as interaction begins to unfold one is more likely to employ low risk patterns of self presentation which cue others on the appropriate response. In addition, the more important a specific self-object relationship is to one, the more blatant the cues for a preferred response. *Third*, after one leaves an interaction, one tends to store and recall favorable evaluations much more often than negative reactions. Self-concept support is much more frequently recalled, with greater discussion than disconfirming communication (Swan and Read 1981).

Self-presentation is accomplished at the discretion of the individual. The individual's impulse to develop a clear and accurate sense of self comes into conflict with his impulse to protect his preferred vision of self. This conflict leads one to carefully choose the self-concept characteristics one presents to whom at what time. One's habitual communicating style in presenting one's self can be characterized as high on risk and low on disclosure. Such habitual styles may be termed conventional, interpersonal, manipulative, and open. In dealing with hostile people one frequently employs a conventional style; in dealing with friendly people one frequently employs an open style. On most occasions one varies the communicating style in such a manner as to obtain positive self-concept support. The strategies for obtaining positive self-concept support vary according to the stages of inter-action. In *initiating* interaction, one seeks out supportive others; in *maintaining* interaction, one patterns the response of others; and in *reflecting* on interaction, one stores and recalls most clearly and accurately positive self-concept support.

The Validation of Individual Self-Concepts

It should be apparent by now that a clear and precise analysis of the processes involved in self-validation turns upon our ability to construct messages such that others *understand* and provide *positive self-concept support* for our specific self-object relationships. From the communicator's point of view, perceived under-standing and perceived self-concept support are central to the validation of one's self-concept.

Perceived Understanding. Throughout our analysis of individual self-concept formation we have attempted to demonstrate that presenting and sustaining a specific self-object relationship depends on an individual's ability (1) to become aware of a range of potential self-object relationships through social role-taking, (2) to select from that range the preferred self-object relationships one wants to appropriate to one's self-concept, and then (3) to present and validate our preferred self-object relationships in the presence of preferred others. However, how does one know when some other, indeed, understands what relationships have been proposed? Recent research by Cahn and his associates (Cahn 1982; Cahn and Shulman 1982) has isolated the specific cues which when presented by a receiver indicate to the sender that a message is understood. The more frequently a listener cues the communicator by verbal or non-verbal signs of the following, the more the communicator will feel understood:

Satisfaction	Acceptance
Relaxation	Comfort
Pleasure	Happiness
Goodness	Importance

One and only one marker is necessary for perceived understanding. However, the more cues perceived when inferring listener responses, the stronger the com-municator's belief that his message is understood.

One does not communicate simply to be understood, but rather to seek a realization regarding what is understood. Perceived understanding indexes the intensity of that realization and thus indexes the communicator's perception of the action he or she expects the listener to follow based on this understanding. There-fore, the degree of consensus a listener is perceived to cue in the understanding of symbolic interaction indicates the likelihood to which the listener is perceived to realize that which is understood.

Perceived understanding while necessary for validating one's self-concept is not in and of itself sufficient for achieving this goal. One must combine perceived understanding with the communication skills required to obtain *perceived self-*

concept support. It is important to know how to convey support for another's self-concept. To do this, however, one must recognize the unique scope, depth, and configuration of another's self-concept *and* must know the communication rules governing how messages purporting to support someone's self-concept are created.

Five dimensions are significant when creating messages to convey self-concept support. An individual can express support for another's identity, evaluative, and behavioral self-object relations. It is also possible to support another's real and ideal self-concept. Messages that seek to convey to another that one has supported his self-concept must manipulate one or more of these dimensions. In the next chapter, we will attempt to demonstrate how support for different combinations of these self-object relationships are instrumental in establishing such interpersonal relationships as pertain between friends and mates, and how different intensities of self-concept support lead to differing intensities of interpersonal relationships such as casual friend, good friend, best friend. However, our task will be to demonstrate empirically that positive self-concept support not only validates one's self-concept but forms the basis for interpersonal attraction.

Wylie (1979), in a critical and comprehensive review of the research on the self-concept, provides strong evidence that perceived self-concept support not only serves to validate others' self-concepts but is an important message variable for creating interpersonal attraction. First, a detailed discussion of 34 studies confirms a significant main effect for manipulated self-regard, or perceived self-concept support, on interpersonal attraction. Next, literature dealing with actual self-concept similarity and attraction, assumed self-concept similarity and attraction, and the interactive effect of actual and assured self-concept similarity on interpersonal attraction was reviewed. The results of 31 of these studies found little empirical support for a relationship between interpersonal attraction and *actual* similarities between the self-concepts of two individuals (Wylie 1979:528). In contrast, the results of 20 studies found the relationship between an individual's assumed self-concept similarities with others and interpersonal attraction to those others was significant and positive (Wylie 1979:535). In all of these studies assumed self-concept similarities were manipulated using communication. Finally, five studies examining the effects of actual and assumed self-concept similarity on interpersonal attraction found actual interpersonal similarity of self-description was *not* related to interpersonal attraction, whereas subjects' assumptions of similarity between own and other's characteristics *were* significantly related to interpersonal attraction (Wylie 1979:537).

In light of the evidence marshalled above, three conclusions seem warranted. First, manipulated self-regard and assumed self-concept similarity, both of which are instances of perceived self-concept support, produced a *positive main effect* on interpersonal attraction. Second, actual self-concept similarity did *not* affect this relationship. Third, perceived self-concept support acted as a message variable capable of being manipulated in terms of its focus and intensity. Further, these manipulations were found to retain their focus and intensity for extended periods of time.

In summary, it has been argued that the manifestation of perceived understanding and perceived self-concept support are necessary and sufficient conditions for self-concept validation. Further, it has been demonstrated that perceived understanding and perceived self-concept support provide the basis for interpersonal attraction, which in turn serves as a basis for all forms of interpersonal relationships. In the next chapter, we shall explore the different types and levels of self-concept understanding and support which form the basis for initiating a variety of interpersonal relationships. We shall then explore how different types of self-concept support lead to different types of interpersonal relationships (e.g., Those between lovers, compared with those between friends or mates), and how different degrees of self-concept support reflect varying gradations of a particular interpersonal role, e.g., acquaintance vs. best friend; casual date vs. mate.

Propositions

1. Self-concept development depends upon an individual's role-taking skills.
2. Basic, reflective, appropriative, and synesic are increased levels of specificity of role-taking.
3. Basic and reflective role-taking apply to the cultural and organizational systems of information about self.
4. Appropriative and synesic role-taking apply to the interpersonal system of information about self.
5. Self-concept presentation aims at obtaining feedback from others on proposed self-object relationships.
6. Communicators develop specific styles of self-concept presentation based upon the degree of risk and disclosure in their messages.
7. Conventional, interpersonal, manipulative and open styles of communication reflect different degrees with risk and disclosure.
8. Communicators normally plan self-presentation so as to obtain positive self-concept support.
9. Self-concept validation requires messages which convey both preferred understanding and preferred self-concept support.
10. Perceived understanding and perceived self-concept support are important message variables in establishing interpersonal attraction.
11. Different types and degrees of understanding and perceived self-concept support lead to differential types and degrees of interpersonal relationships.

References

Cahn, D.D. Uptake Acts: Discourse Analytic Markers for Perceived Understanding. Paper: Summer Conference on Language and Discourse Processes. Michigan State University, E. Lansing, MI, 1982.

Cahn, D.D., and Shulman, G.M. The Measurement of the Perception of Being Understood/ Misunderstood: Development and Assessment. Paper: Central States Speech Association Convention, Milwaukee, WI, 1982.

Cushman, D.P., and Craig, R.T. Communication Systems: Interpersonal Implications. In G.R. Miller (Ed.) *Explorations in Interpersonal Communication*. ed. G.R. Miller, 37–58. Beverly Hills, CA: Sage Publications, 1976.

Cushman, D.P., and Florence, T. The Development of Interpersonal Communication Theory. *Today's Speech*. 22:11–15, 1974.

Lauer, R.H., and Boardman, L. Role-taking: Theory, Topology and Propositions. *Sociology and Social Research*. 55, 137-148, 1971.

Mead, G.H. *Mind, Self, and Society*. Chicago, IL: University of Chicago Press 1934.

Norton, R.W. Foundations of a Communicator Style Construct. *Human Communication Research*. 4:99–112, 1978.

Swann, Jr., W.B., and Read, S. Self-Verification Processes: How We Sustain our Self-Conceptions. *Journal of Experimental Social Psychology*. 17:351–372, 1981.

Wylie, R.C. *The Self-Concept*. Lincoln: University of Nebraska Press, 1979.

4

Interpersonal Communication and the Formation and Maintenance of Interpersonal Relationships

> To separate out my relationship to myself and set it aside for more luxuriant attention may be pleasurable, it may even be useful, but like any surgery it becomes more dangerous the longer it lasts. I am immobilized and temporarily severed from the other half of life. Ultimately my character is defined by the quality of my sensitivity to other people. I exist in equilibrium. I am here to the degree I am there.
>
> Hugh Prather (1977:10)

Interpersonal Relationships

Human communication is, as we have seen, a complex enterprise which has come to the forefront as a major problem of the age. Equally intriguing, and at times even more mystifying, are processes by which individuals employ human communication to establish, maintain, and terminate interpersonal relationships. The problem of explaining the role communication plays in interpersonal relationships has recently emerged as one of the chief challenges to social scientific research and as such has attracted the attention of scholars across a wide variety of disciplines.

Information regarding such relationships is important for several reasons. First, Campbell et al. (1976) found that people identify interpersonal relationships more than anything else as making their lives meaningful. Second, several researchers have found the failure of interpersonal relationships to be correlated with such important social problems as suicide (Stech 1980), psychiatric abnormality (Bloom, Asher, and White 1978), social stress (Chiriboga 1979) and family stability (Albrecht 1980). Third, numerous studies demonstrate that effective communication is one of the key variables in sustaining successful interpersonal relationships (Alexander 1973; Norton and Glick 1976: Murstein 1972), while its absence is a key variable in causing the failure of such relationships (Alexander 1973; Norton and Glick 1976).

The processes involved in initiating and maintaining an interpersonal relationship involve both an affective and a practical component. The affective component normally takes some form of liking or loving. The practical component takes the form of a three stage filtering process. In this latter case people tend to associate with those whose social, economic and educational status is similar to their own. These status characteristics limit the range and type of people one meets. Such characteristics determine one's *field of available* interactions. Similarly, within one's field of available interactions there will exist a subset of people whom, as a result of initial interaction, one finds interesting and whom one wishes to approach in order to initiate a more intimate type of interpersonal relationship. Such individuals form a *field of approachables*. Finally, within the field of approachables, there exists a subset of people who find others interesting and desirable for forming relationships. Such individuals constitute a *field of reciprocals* (Cushman, Valentinsen, and Dietrich 1982).

Previously we attempted to demonstrate that the manifestation of perceived self-concept support leads to interpersonal attraction, and that such attraction was a necessary basis for forming interpersonal relationships. Similarly, we suggested that differential types and intensities of reciprocal self-concept support lead to different types of interpersonal relationships (e.g., with friends or with mates) and to different intensities of a given relationship (e.g., one may have a casual friend, a good friend, and a best friend). It will be the purpose of this chapter to explore the role self-concept support plays within our three-stage filtering process in initiating and maintaining two types of interpersonal relationships. More specifically, we shall explore the types of self-concept support involved in (1) initiating and maintaining relationships with friends and (2) initiating and maintaining relationships with a mate.

The Friendship Formation Process

Few interpersonal relationships are more important to a person and to the development of an accurate and secure sense of self than friendships. Researchers tell us that individuals have an average number of four close friends, and that generally one of these is a member of the opposite sex (Booth 1972). This research will also indicate that each year you will meet between ten and fifteen people with whom you would like to initiate friendly relationships, and that about half of these individuals will choose not to be friends with you. In addition, each year one or more of our close friends will change interaction patterns, move away, or die, leaving an empty space in our lives, and provoking a search for someone to fill the void (Booth and Hess 1974).

While such empirical descriptions are informative in that they tell us how similar or different we are from most Americans, in the past they have indicated little about the quality of life created by interaction with a friend. These studies told us even less about how friendships are formed and sustained in interaction. Recently, however, this trend has changed with several researchers in a variety of disciplines directing their attention to (1) the essential qualities of friendship, (2) the type of perceptions which provoke the initiation of a friendly relationship and (3) the type of interaction patterns which sustain and deepen friendship.

Based upon the work of several researchers, there appear to be three underlying dimensions of friendship formation: trust, self-concept support, and helping behavior (La Gaipa 1972; Crawford 1977; Gibbs 1977). Trust refers to a relationship based upon authenticity; self-concept support refers to a relationship based on respect for one's social and psychological self; helping behavior refers to a relationship based upon reciprocal assistance in time of need. Friends appear to be reliably classifiable, in terms of increasing levels of intensity, as acquaintances, casual friends, good friends, and best friends, based upon increasing levels of trust, self-concept support, and helping behaviors. In addition, friendship appears to fulfill the need for two types of roles, confidant and companion. A confidant is someone who provides evaluative self-concept support, while a companion is someone who provides behavioral self-concept support. The same friend may fill either one or both of these roles.

While a clear pattern emerges from the research literature regarding underlying dimensions and levels of friendship, the process by which one selects and sustains such relationships is far from clear. Cushman, Valentinsen, and Dietrich (1982) model friendship formation as a three-stage process. At each stage a different set of factors influences friendship formation by filtering out certain individuals. The three stages will allow one to identify an individual's field of available, approach-able, and reciprocal friends.

Field of Availables. To begin with, we have a set of causal and normative forces which interact to determine our field of availables. Although one meets an inde-terminately large number of people in one's lifetime, several biological and social forces combine to causally and normatively constrain whom one is likely to en-counter. Such causal forces as birth and death rates, as well as the age and sexual distributions of a population, serve to constrain the field of availables (Hacker 1979). Similarly, such normative forces as a society's social, educational, religious, and economic structures, as well as socialization processes and role distribution patterns, serve to further constrain whom one is likely to encounter (Booth 1972). The process of communicative interaction in the field of availables and the prin-ciples governing these interactions have already been well delineated by Berger and Calabrese (1975) and Duck (1976) in their investigations of initial social interactions. It only needs to be stressed here that those investigations show the communication rules governing such interactions to be standardized and general across individuals.

Field of Approachables. Within one's field of availables there will exist a subset of individuals whom as a result of initial interaction one finds desirable and would consider approaching in order to initiate a friendship. This subset of people con-stitutes one's field of approachables. Three normative rules delimit one's field of approachables and thus form the basis for the interpersonal interaction rules that govern and guide friendship initiation. The first two rules specify the individual perceptions that form the antecedent conditions for creating messages aimed at establishing a friendly relationship. The value of these antecedent perceptions is determined by the information an individual obtains in initial interaction with the field of availables. The third rule specifies the content of messages that when presented will be perceived by others as an attempt to establish a friend relationship.

(1) *The greater an individual's perceived relationship between positive attributes of his own self-concept and the perceived attributes of another's self-concept, the greater the likelihood he or she will attempt to initiate communication arrived at by supporting those similar attributes.* More specifically, when I think there are qualities of your self-concept that I enjoy because they are similar to qualities I admire in my self-concept, then I will attempt to support your self-concept by telling you how much I approve of those specific self-object relationships. Needless to say, the more self-object commonalities we have, the more self-concept support I will provide for you (Thompson and Nishimura 1952; Lundy 1956, 1958; Elman, Press and Rosenkrantz 1970).

(2) *The greater an individual's perceived likelihood that the other will accept an offer of self-concept support, the greater the likelihood that communication will be initiated.* More specifically, when I think that you are likely to respond favorably to my offer of self-concept support I am more likely to provide such support (Laumann 1969).

(3) *The more frequently an individual provides messages that support some positive identity, evaluative, or behavioral self-object relationships of another's self-concept, the greater the likelihood that the other person will perceive those messages as an attempt to initiate a friend relationship.* More specifically, the more frequently I provide self-concept support to you, the greater the possibility you will think I want to be your friend.

In summary, if I think there are real, ideal, identity, evaluative and behavioral self-object relationships in your self-concept that I respect because they are also a part of my own real or ideal self-concept, then I will attempt to initiate a friendship with you by conveying through communication my support for you in regard to those self-object relationships.

Field of Reciprocals. As Laumann (1969) clearly indicates, not all attempts at establishing relationships are reciprocated. Rather, within one's field of approachables there exists a subset of individuals who will make up one's list of actual friends, one's field of reciprocals. Two normative rules delimit one's field of reciprocals and thus form the basis for the interpersonal interaction rules which govern and guide the process of friendship growth.

(1) *The greater an individual's perceived accuracy with regard to the similarity between one's own and another's self-concept, the greater the likelihood that a friend relationship will grow.* Put another way, the more frequently my interactions with you reveal the accuracy of my initial perceptions of the portions of your self-concept I respect, the greater the likelihood our relationship will grow (Laumann 1969; Duck 1973).

(2) *The greater the reciprocated self-concept support, the greater the likelihood that a friend relationship will grow.* More specifically, the greater the respect we manifest for each other's self-concept, the greater the likelihood our relationship will grow (Bailey, Finney and Helm 1975; Bailey, Digiacomo and Zinser 1976).

In summary, if I am accurate in my original perceptions of my respect for your self-concept, and if that respect expands and is reciprocated, then self-concept support will increase, causing the relationship to deepen and grow.

What then can we conclude regarding our understanding of the friend relationship and how it is initiated and maintained? Intuitively, it seems, we have always known that true friendship . . . the kind of intimate trust and mutual respect between individuals in which each is free to reveal his or her deepest feelings to others or to seek and obtain support and companionship . . . is one of the most beautiful and meaningful aspects of human existence. Our analysis has attempted to take this intuition and reveal what scientific research suggests are two components of such a relationship and then to draw out some implications of this research for initiating and maintaining friendship through communication. We discovered that friendship appears to have several rather specific underlying components. An important and essential factor in all levels of friendship is trust or authenticity. Another important and essential factor is self-concept support or respect for certain specific relationships between a friend and other objects or persons. Finally, an important and essential factor at all levels of friendship is the kind of affection which manifests itself in helping behaviors. The more an individual manifests these underlying factors, the more likely a relationship is to become deeper, to proceed from acquaintance to intimacy.

We then noted that three communication rules regulate the initiation of a "friend-relationship". The first two rules indicate the perceptions one must have from previous interaction in order for one to initiate a proposal of friendship in the current interaction. The third rule regulates what one must say in order to initiate a friend-relationship. We argued that when an individual perceives (1) that some other's self-concept is similar in self-object relationships to one's own real or ideal self and (2) that the other is likely to accept one's support of that self-object relationship, then one will send messages conveying self-concept support for those specific self-object relationships, and his or her actions will be viewed by the other as an attempt to initiate a friend-relationship. The more self-object relationships one supports in another's self-concept and the greater the intensity of that support (the practical process), the greater the potential for that friendship to grow and deepen (the affective process).

While self-concept support is essential in order to initiate a friend-relationsip, if that potential is to be realized, the other must reciprocate such a proposal of friendship. Two communication rules seem to guide the maintenance of such a reciprocal act. A friendship will grow and deepen in direct proportion to (1) the accuracy of the supported self-object relationship and (2) the reciprocal self-concept support provided by the other individual. Typically, such reciprocated friendship evolves into a *confidant* role if one is *supporting evaluative self-object* relationships, a *companion* role if one is *supporting behavioral self-object* relationships, and both if one is supporting both types of relationship.

Finally, a word must be said about the difference between authentic self-concept support and its imitator, mere flattery. Perhaps all that can be said about the difference between those two types of communication is captured in this quotation from Prather:

> I have a friend who is a good listener. If I tell her about some difficulty I am having, I never get the feeling she is doing little more than waiting to say something supportive. Her primary concern is not to put on a show of being a good listener, but rather it is as though my problem has become her problem in all respects. She is intensely loyal and yet she does not automatically criticize the one I may be blaming. She has an instinct for knowing how much I love that person, and if I do she speaks gently because she is for me; by that I mean she wants for me what I want at the deepest level, and she knows when my anger is superficial. However, if the person is not significant to my life, her criticism so devours him that by the time she is through I can laugh at my foolishness for having exaggerated his importance.
>
> (Prather 1977:11)

We can illustrate our analysis of the friendship formation process through an application of the Twenty Question Statement Test. Below are summaries of the Twenty Statement Tests done on each of four individuals. Each of these four summaries was contructed from three actual tests done on the people listed (one on themselves and two by others on them). The summaries then contain only each person's *real self-concept*. Since all of those people are considered by Lee to be friends, we shall analyze them one at a time in comparison with Lee to see if we can detect why they are friends and how close they are.

First, let us explore the relationship between Lee and Don. We begin by noting their self-concept similarities, since according to our first rule these similarities will indicate the potential basis for a friend-relationship. Note the similarity of these real self-concepts at the *basic level* . . . professor and teacher, at the *reflective level* . . . likes travel and likes good food, at the *appropriate level* . . . assertive and talkative and at the *synesic level* . . . helpful and thoughtful. The potential for reciprocal self-concept support between Lee and Don is substantial and involves the cultural and organizational communication systems in their basic and reflective self-concept qualities and the interpersonal communication system in their appropriate and synesic self-concept qualities. In addition, the fact that they are both talkative and assertive as well as thoughtful and helpful suggests a high likelihood of both giving and accepting the other's self-concept support. In addition, since these are real-self concepts, or self-object relationships which all who interact with them pick-up in interaction, it seems likely that the commonalities between them will be accurately perceived. Finally, since these two self-concepts have so much similarity and that similarity exists at each level with the role-taking process, their respect for one another has a great potential to grow and deepen. This is a classic instance of two individuals who have a great potential to provide the kind of self-concept support which creates a relationship of best friend.

Table 6

Twenty Question Statement Test on

Lee and Three of his Friends

Lee's Real Self		Don's Real Self		Bill's Real Self		Sue's Real Self	
1. Professor	B	Intelligent	A	Professor	B	Mystical	A
2. Married	A	Assertive	A	Researcher	B	Professor	B
3. Teacher	B	Talkative	A	Status Conscious	A	Teacher	B
4. Researcher	B	Helpful	S	Meek	A	Married	A
5. Likes good food	R	Thoughtful	S	Insecure	A	Friendly	S
6. Likes travel	R	Professor	B	Dislikes criticism	R	Helpful	S
7. Assertive	A	Teacher	B	Intelligent	A	Likes good food	R
8. Helpful	S	Researcher	B	Dislikes conflict	R	Likes wild clothes	R
9. Talkative	A	Likes travel	R	Concerned	S	Unsure	A
10. Thoughtful	S	Likes good food	R	Friendly	S	Happy	A
etc.		etc.		etc.		etc.	

A = Appropriative   R = Reflective

B = Basic   S = Synesic

Second, let us explore the relationship between Lee and Sue. Note the similarity of self-concepts at the *basic level* . . . professor and teacher, at the *reflective level* . . . likes good food, at the *appropriative level* . . . married and at the *synesic level* . . . helpful. The potential for reciprocal self-concept support is less than in the case of Lee and Don, but still present in the cultural, organizational, and inter-personal systems of communication. Both self-concepts reflect helping behavior, one of the important qualities of friendship, and thus will likely offer each other positive self-concept support. Again, because of the real self-concept similarity we can expect high accuracy in their perceptions of each other. These two people have a potential casual friend-relationship.

Third, let us explore the relationship between Lee and Bill. Note the similarity of self-*reflective level* . . . none; the *appropriative level* . . . none; and the *synesic level* . . . none. Here Lee, because he is talkative, thoughtful and helpful, may provide self-concept support for Bill at the basic level, but will probably get little or none from Bill who is meek and status conscious. In addition, Lee's assertiveness may cause Bill problems since he is status conscious, meek, insecure, and dislikes criticism. These two people have the potential for only a minimal level of friendship such as acquaintance and at the basic role-taking level of co-workers. These two self-concepts severely constrain the ability of these people to become interpersonal friends and for that friendship to grow without significant self-concept change.

You may wish to try such an analysis on your friendship group. If you do, keep the following in mind. First, use *real* rather than ideal self-concept summaries to ensure accuracy for self-concept support. Second, pay attention to those appropriate and synesic qualities that affect interaction (like talkative) and affect friendship (like helpful).

Now that we have considered the interpersonal communication rules that govern and guide the initiation and growth of friendship relations, we shall direct our attention to the same processes with respect to mates.

The Mate Formation Process

Technically, the term mate refers to any opposite sex relationship for which one clears the field of competitors. Such a relationship normally includes a major portion of individuals who are going steady, engaged, cohabiting, or married. *Practically*, the term mate refers to some other for whom we feel a deep sense of *love and commitment*. "Mate-relationships" account for a great deal of the intense happiness, satisfaction, and meaning one finds in life, and function as strong integrating forces which serve to temper the selfishness one feels from time to time. The idea that love and commitment represent strong integrative forces in human relationships has always been difficult for scientific researchers to deal with. *Love appears to be* an integrating force in a relationship, a force which exerts its effect through "socialization to the beliefs that one's concern for the welfare of the other, one's helping the other, one's concern for being with the other, one's pain in the absence of the other, and one's dependency on the other are key attributes of an intimate relationship" (Krain 1977:250). *Commitment appears to be* a focusing force in a relationship, a force which directs one's interest in affection toward a particular person to the exclusion of others (Karp, Jackson and Lester 1970). While such practical feelings and intentions have been fairly commonplace regarding a mate-relationship, only recently has scientific research in a variety of disciplines began to reveal (1) the essential underlying qualities involved in "mateships", (2) the types of perceptions which provoke initiation of mate-relationships and (3) the type of interaction patterns required to deepen and sustain such a relationship.

Because the mate process, situation, or context is different from that of friendship, the communication rules are different. Based upon the work of several researchers, the specific types of love and commitment involved in a mate-relationship appear to differ from that of other types of interpersonal relationships by the manner in which intelligence, physical attraction, sex appear, affection, and ideal "mateness" affect the relationship (Pam, Plutchik and Conte 1973). When one is selecting a mate, one is attracted most to others of the opposite sex whom one believes are about as intelligent, physically attractive, and sexually appealing as one thinks one is. One is also attracted to others whom one believes fit one's ideal of what constitutes a good mate, whether those ideals are culturally or individually formed. The closer someone of the opposite sex comes to one's ideal conception of a mate, the more likely one is to clear the field and feel a commitment to the relationship. Finally, one is attracted most to others of the opposite sex who reciprocate expressions of affection based on the previously discussed qualities.

The more one believes that the other is an ideal mate and will reciprocate affection, the more one will move from a casual date to a steady date, to a fiance, to a spouse. We shall explore the processes involved in initiating and maintaining a mate-relationship within the three-stage filtering process previously discussed.

Field of Availables. In addition to the previously discussed causal and normative forces which constrain the field of available friends, mates are further influenced by the individual's view of marriage, the divorce rate, and the number of individuals whose mates die.

Field of Approachables. Within one's field of availables, there exists a subset of individuals whom one finds desirable and would consider approaching in order to initiate a mate-relationship. This subset constitutes one's field of approachables. Five normative rules define one's field of approachables and thus form the basis for the interpersonal interaction rules which govern the initiation style. The first four rules specify the perceptions one must obtain from prior interaction in order to consider initiating a mate relationship. The fifth rule prescribes what you must say in order to be understood as proposing such a relationship.

(1) *The greater an individual's perception that a member of the opposite sex is as intelligent, physically attractive, and sexually appealing as one thinks one is, the greater the likelihood of initiating communication aimed at establishing a mate-relationship.* More specifically, if my previous interactions with someone of the opposite sex tell me that he or she is about as smart, good looking, and sexually attractive as I am, then I feel both at ease and suffiently attracted to that individual to attempt to establish a mate-relationship (Cavior and Boblett 1972; Hill, Rubin and Peplau 1976; Murstein 1972; Berschied and Walster 1973).

(2) *The greater an individual's perception that someone of the opposite sex has a real self-concept similar to one's ideal-self for a mate, the greater the likelihood of initiating communication aimed at establishing a mate-relationship.* For example, I may ideally want as a mate someone who is thoughtful, easy to be with, and likes living in the country. After having met you and decided that you are about as intelligent, physically attractive, and sexually appealing as I am, I note that your real self-object relationships are exactly what I ideally want (Bailey and Helm 1974; Murstein 1972; Luckey 1960).

(3) *The greater an individual's perception that the male's real-ideal self-concept discrepancy is small, the greater the likelihood of initiating communication aimed at establishing a mate-relationship.* More specifically, it is only when a man is very close to what he would like to be that he seriously considers a mate-relationship. Moreover, it is only when a woman also believes that a man is what he would like to be that she considers him suffiently stable and clears the field of competition. However, for women the requirement of a similar low real-ideal self discrepancy does not appear essential based on the research done thus far (Luckey 1962; Murstein 1972).

(4) *The greater an individual's perception that someone of the opposite sex is likely to accept one's offer of a relationship, the greater the likelihood of initiating communication aimed at establishing a mate-relationship.* Both common sense and

scientific research note the retarding effect of one's perception that one might be turned down on the initiation of such a relationship. (Shantean and Nagy 1979; Huston 1973; Murstein 1972).

(5) *The more frequently an individual (a) provides messages that manifest self-concept support for someone of the opposite sex's intelligence, physical attraction, and sex appeal; (b) characterizes that person as fulfilling his or her role of an ideal mate and (c) indicates a perceived lack of discrepancy between the mate's real and ideal self, the greater the likelihood that the other individual will perceive those messages as an attempt to initiate a mate-relationship.* In short, initiating a mate-relationship depends upon my perceiving that you have the above mentioned self-object relationships and communicating my self-concept support to you for them.

Field of Reciprocals. Within one's field of approachables exists a subset of individuals who will reciprocate one's offer of a mate relationship when the occasion arises. Two normative rules influence when individuals chose to reciprocate an offer and these form the basis for two interaction rules for establishing and maintaining a mate-relationship.

(1) *The greater the accuracy in relevant self-object relationships, the greater the likelihood the relationship will grow.* More specifically, if in fact my perceptions of self-object relationships in regard to mateship for another are accurate, then I will continue my self-concept support, and our relationship will grow (Luckey 1960, a and b; Murstein 1971, 1972; Schafer, Braito and Bohlen 1973).

(2) *The greater the perception that there is reciprocation of self-concept support in regard to the mate selection rules, the greater the likelihood the relationship will grow.* Reciprocated affection is essential to relational growth (Byrne and Blaylock 1963; Bailey and Mettetal 1977; Luckey 1962).

What then can we conclude regarding our understanding of the mate-relationship and how it is initiated and maintained? Intuition and common sense tell us that entering into a mate-relationship is a serious and challenging decision which, as research shows, requires an intense feeling of love and commitment. Both of these factors involve a balancing of ideal and real components. One's perception that another has a certain amount of intelligence, physical attraction, and sex appeal must be real enough to sustain a relationship and ideal enough to allow for the rationalization of individual mistakes, blemishes, and differences in arousals. One's perception that another is an ideal-mate must be real enough to sustain a relationship and yet ideal enough to allow for another's individuality in the midst of relatedness. Considerable research reveals the presence and necessity of both an idealization and a reality component in order to maintain the intensity of love and the intensity of commitment necessary for the mate-relationship (Hall and Taylor 1976; Kephart 1967). It is perhaps for this reason more than any, that going steady, cohabiting, and marriage have a public component, a symbolic act which others can observe, such as an exchange of pins, a setting up of a common household, or a legal declaration of marriage as a constraint upon taking one's vows of love and commitment too lightly. Hugh Prather put the point this way:

I looked at long-term marriages with suspicion. After all, how much change could ten or twenty years with the same person allow? And when there is little variation, little stimulation, people are predisposed to remain as they are. Now my experience has shown me an alternative, and like many other things that work, it doesn't argue well. I am quite certain that Gayle and I would not be together now if we had not consented to, or had not constructed for ourselves, some type of deterrence to leaving. By getting married, we agreed to try for something lasting; we agreed to rules that would make parting unpleasant; we pledged love, support, and equal sharing of all that we had; and we declared this publicly so that if we failed it would be known. It was not a reasonable thing to do.

(Prather 1977:51)

We can again illustrate our previous analysis of the mate formation process through an application of the Twenty Question Test. Below are summaries of the Twenty Statement Tests done on each of four individuals. These four individuals represent two couples. In this case, the Twenty Question Statement Tests include both real *and* ideal self statements from one other person besides the couples themselves. This allows us to locate self-object relationships which are real to the couples but not to a third person. Such relationships are labeled ideal even though they exist for the couple. Real self-concept qualities exist for all three people filling out the tests.

First, let us examine the relationship between Jim and Sue. We may begin by noting that this relationship has a potential for reciprocal self-concept support in regard to *intelligence* . . . both see Sue as educated, and both view Jim as intelligent; *physical attraction* . . . both call Sue attractive and both view Jim as handsome; and *sexually appealing* . . . both see Sue as sexy, and both view Jim as sexy. Note that several of these characteristics, while common to Jim and Sue's relationship, are ideal self-concept qualities when one adds a third person to the evaluation. It also seems apparent that Jim's real and ideal self-discrepancy may be large in that he is indecisive and dissatisfied. There is little evidence that either person is viewed by the other as an ideal-mate; both are primarily appropriative individuals with only one synesic quality. However, their appropriative characteristics fit together well and this guarantees self-concept support. Since this relationship lacks (a) a low real-ideal self-discrepancy in the male, and (b) evidence of ideal mateness on both sides, then the relationship has the potential for only a casual date. In addition, Sue's assertiveness, strength, and talkativeness will in the long run further erode Jim's confidence, which is already characterized as indecisive and dissatisfying.

Second, let us examine Bob and Jan's relationship. Here again self-concept support is potentially high in regard to *intelligence* . . . Bob is a professor, and Jan is intelligent; *physically attractive* . . . Bob is good looking, and Jan is attractive; and *sexually appealing* . . . Bob is sexy, and Jan is sexy. Again, Jan's intelligence and Bob's physical attraction are unique to their relationship (ideal

Table 7

Twenty Questions Statement Test on Two Couples

COUPLE ONE		COUPLE TWO	
Jim's self-concept	Sue's self-concept	Bob's self-concept	Jan's self-concept
1. intelligent - Appropriative (I)	1. strong - Appropriative (R)	1. good looking - Appropriative (I)	1. intelligent - Appropriative (I)
2. assertive - Appropriative (R)	2. attractive - Appropriative (R)	2. sexy - Appropriative (I)	2. insecure - Appropriative (R)
3. indecisive - Appropriative (R)	3. educated - Appropriative (R)	3. caring - Synesic (R)	3. attractive - Appropriative (R)
4. critical - Appropriative (R)	4. talkative - Appropriative (R)	4. stable - Appropriative (R)	4. nurse - Basic (R)
5. insightful - Appropriative (R)	5. assertive - Appropriative (R)	5. professor - Appropriative (R)	5. quiet - Appropriative (R)
6. challenging - Appropriative (R)	6. hard-working - Appropriative (R)	6. talkative - Appropriative (R)	6. caring - Synesic (R)
7. handsome - Appropriative (I)	7. sexy - Appropriative (I)	7. helpful - Synesic (R)	7. likes dancing - Reflective (R)
8. sensitive - Synesic (R)	8. creative - Appropriative (R)	8. hardworking - Appropriative (R)	8. likes travel - Reflective (R)
9. sexy - Appropriative (I)	9. firm - Appropriative (R)	9. likes dancing - Reflective (R)	9. sexy - Appropriative (I)
10. dissatisfied - Appropriative (R)	10. sensitive - Synesic (R)	10. likes travel - Reflective (R)	10. supportive - Synesic (R)
etc. . . .	etc. . . .	etc.	etc. . . .

(I) ideal self-concept
(R) real self-concept

self). Bob's real and ideal appear to be close, since he is stable. Again very little evidence is present of ideal mateship. The match in reflective, appropriative, and synesic qualities suggest there will be a substantial potential for reciprocal self-concept support. Since both are caring persons, we also have a strong potential for reciprocal affection, with nine of the ten self-statements listed as real self-concept qualities. There is high accuracy and some idealization, although this is small. This relationship has the potential to lead to going steady, cohabiting, or maybe even marriage if both begin to take the other more seriously as an ideal mate. However, with Jan's intelligence being an ideal characteristic unique to the relationship and her being insecure with little idealization of herself by Bob, there is some potential for the erosion of Jan's self as intelligent. Still Bob is caring and helpful, so perhaps not.

You may wish to try such an analysis on either couples you know or your own relationship with someone of the opposite sex. Keep the following in mind: partners must do a test on themselves and another on their partners. This will tell you who you are to each other and what is real to the relationship. Then get one other person to do a test on each of you to see what real qualities are also ideal when the other is added. Also be careful of self-concept qualities which are capable of producing conflict in the relationship.

Taken together, our interpersonal relationships with our friends and mates are for most of us the most important and powerful influences in our lives. Such relationships represent the richness of life in that they influence who we are, what we can become, and with whom we share our accomplishments and defeats. The growth of such relationships is an exciting and beautiful adventure. The disintegration of such relationships can be difficult to cope with and tragic in its consequences. This chapter has attempted to outline the communication process involved in the formation and growth of interpersonal relationships. Our next chapter will explore the issues and communication patterns involved in assessing interpersonal relationships in order to escalate their effects on the individuals involved.

Propositions

1. The processes involved in initiating and maintaining an interpersonal relationship may be viewed as a three stage filtering process involving: (a) one's field of availables, (b) one's field of approachables, and (c) one's field of reciprocals.
2. Different types and intensities of self-concept support lead to different types and intensities of interpersonal relationships.
3. Trust, self-concept support, and helping behavior appear to be the underlying dimensions of intimacy in friendship.
4. Friendship appears to be reliably classifiable into increasing levels of intensity; the relationships that obtain between acquaintances, between casual friends, good friends, and best friends typify these levels of intensity.

5. The greater an individual's perceived relationship between attributes of his or her own self-concept and the perceived attributes of another's self-concept, the greater the likelihood that he or she will attempt to initiate a friend-relationship through communication arrived at supporting those similar attributes.

6. The more likely it seems to an individual that another will accept his or her offer of friendship, the more likely it is that communication will be initiated.

7. The more frequently an individual provides messages that support some positive identity, evaluative, or behavioral self-object relationship of another's self-concept, the greater the likelihood that the other will perceive those messages as an attempt to initiate a friend relationship.

8. The more accurately one perceives the similarity between one's own and another's self-concept, the greater the likelihood that a friend-relationship will grow.

9. The greater the reciprocated self-concept support, the greater the likelihood that a friend-relationship will grow.

10. Typically, self-concept support for an evaluative self-object relationship leads to a friendship role of confidant, while support for a behavioral self-object relationship leads to a friendship role of companion, and support for both leads to a combined friendship role.

11. Authentic self-concept support can be separated from mere flattery in that it reflects a sensitive understanding of how the specific self-object relationship being supported fits into the other's larger self.

12. Love appears to be an integrating force, while commitment is a focusing of forces in the mate-relationship.

13. Intelligence, physical attraction, sex appeal, ideal mate, closeness between the male's real and ideal self, and reciprocated affection represent the underlying dimensions of a mate-relationship.

14. Mateship appears to be reliably classifiable into increasing levels of intensity: casual date, steady date, fiancée/fiancé and spouse.

15. The more strongly one perceives someone of the opposite sex to be about as intelligent, physically attractive, and sexually appealing as oneself, the greater the likelihood of initiating communication aimed at establishing a mate-relationship.

16. The greater one's perception that someone of the opposite sex has a real-self concept similar to one's ideal-self for a mate, the greater the likelihood of initiating communication aimed at establishing a mate-relationship.

17. The greater an individual's perception that the male's real-ideal self-concept discrepancy is small, the greater the likelihood of initiating communication aimed at establishing a mate-relationship.

18. The greater one's perception that a person of the opposite sex is likely to accept one's offer of a relationship, the greater the likelihood of initiating communication aimed at establishing a mate-relationship.

19. The more frequently an individual provides messages that manifest self-concept support for another's underlying dimensions with mateship, the greater the likelihood that the other individual will perceive those messages to be an attempt to initiate a mate-relationship.

20. The greater the accuracy in relevant self-object relationships, the greater the likelihood a mate-relationship will grow.

21. The greater the perception that there is reciprocation of self-concept support in regard to the mate selection rules, the greater the likelihood the relationship will grow.

Note

1. Portions of this chapter were taken from Cushman, D.P., Valentinsen, B. and Dietrich, D., A Rules Theory of Interpersonal Relationship. In F.X. Dance. *Comparative Theories of Human Communication*, ed.L New York, NY: Harper Row, 1982.

References

Albrecht, S.L. Reactions and Adjustments to Divorce: Differences in the Experience of Males and Females. *Family Relations.* 29:59–68, 1980.

Alexander, J.F. Defensive and Supportive Communication in Normal and Deviant Families. *Journal of Consulting and Clinical Psychology.* 40:223–31, 1973.

Bailey, R.C., and Helm, B. Matrimonial Commitment and Date/Ideal-date Perceptions. *Perceptual and Motor Skills.* 39:1245–46, 1974.

Bailey, R.C., and Mettetal, G.W., Perceived Intelligence in Married Partners. *Social Behavior and Personality.* 5:137–41, 1977.

Bailey, R.C., Digiacomo, R.J., and Zinser, O. Length of Male and Female Friendship and Perceived Intelligence in Self and Friend. *Journal of Personality Assessment.* 40:635–40, 1976.

Bailey, R.C., Finney, P., and Bailey, K.G. Level of Self-acceptance and Perceived Intelligence in Self and Friend. *Journal of Genetic Psychology.* 124:61–67, 1974.

Bailey, R.C., Finney, P., and Helm, B. Self-concept Support and Friendship. *Journal of Social Psychology.* 96:237–43, 1975.

Berger, C., and Calabrese, R. Some Explorations in Initial Interaction and Beyond: Toward a Developmental Theory of Interpersonal Communication. *Human Communication Research.* 99–112, 1, 1975.

Berschied, E., and Walster, E. Physical Attractiveness. In L. Berkowitz *Advances in Experimental Social Psychology;* ed. New York, NY: Academic Press, 1973.

Bloom, B.L., Asher, S.J., and White, S.W., Marital Disruption as a Stressor: A Review and Analysis. *Psychological Bulletin.* 85:867–94, 1978.

Booth, A. Sex and Social Participation. *Amercian Sociological Review.* 37:183–92, 1972.

Booth, A., and Hess, E. Cross-sex Friendship. *Journal of Marriage and the Family.* 36, 1974.

Byrne, D., and Blaylock, B. Similarity and Assumed Similarity of Attitudes Between Husbands and Wives. *Journal of Abnormal and Social Psychology.* 67:636–40, 1963.

Campbell, A., Converse, P.E., and Rogers, W.L. *The Quality of American Life.* Russel Sage Foundation, New York, N.Y.:1976.

Cavior, N., and Boblett, P. Physical Attractiveness of Dating Versus Married Couples. *Proceedings of the 80th Annual Convention of the American Psychological Association.* 175–76, 1972.

Chiriboga, D.A. Marital Separation and Stress: A Life Course Perspective. *Alternative Life Style.* 2:465–70, 1979.

Crawford, M. What is a Friend? *New Society.* 42:116–17. October, 1977.

Cushman, D.P., Brenner, D., and Valentinsen, B. Three Experimental Manipulations of Perceived Self-concept Support in Interpersonal Relationships. Albany, NY: SUNY, forthcoming.

Cushman, D.P., Valentinsen, B., and Dietrich, D. A Rules Theory of Interpersonal Relationships. In *Comparative Theories of Human Communication,* ed. F.X. Dance, New York, NY: Harper-Row, 1982.

Duck, S. Similarity and Perceived Similarity of Personal Constructs as Influencers of Friendship Choice. *British Journal of Social and Clinical Psychology.* 12:1–6, 1973.

Duck, S. Interpersonal Communication in Developing Acquaintances. In *Exploration in Interpersonal Communication,* ed. G.R. Miller, 127–45. Beverly Hills, CA: Sage Publications, 1976.

Elman, J., Press, A., and Rosenkrantz, S. Sex Roles and Selfconcepts: Real and Ideal. *Proceedings of the 78th Annual Convention of the American Psychological Association.* 455–56, 1970.

Gibbs, S. A Comparative Analysis of Friendship Functions in Six Age Groups of Men and Women. Diss. Wayne State University, Detroit, Michigan, 1977.

Hacker, A. Divorce a la Mode. *New York Review of Books.* 23–30, May, 1979.

Hall, J.A., and Taylor, S. E. When Love is Blind. *Human Relations.* 29:751–761, 1976.

Hill, C.T., Rubin, Z., and Peplau, L.A. Breakups Before Marriage: The End of 103 Affairs. *Journal of Social Issues.* 32:147–68, 1976.

Huston, T.L. Ambiguity of Acceptance, Social Desirability, and Dating Choice. *Journal of Experimental Social Psychology.* 9:32–42, 1973.

Karp, E.S., Jackson, J.H., and Lester, D. Ideal-self Fulfillment in Mate Selection: A Corollary to the Complementary Need *Theory of Mate Selection. Journal of Marriage and the Family.* 32:269–272, 1970.

Kephart, W. Some Correlates of Romantic Love. *Journal of Marriage and the Family.* August, 29:470–74, 1967.

Krain, M. Effects of Love and Liking in Premarital Dyads. *Sociological Focus.* 10:249–62, 1977.

La Gaipa, J.J. Testing a Multidimensional Approach to Friendship. In *Theory and Practice in Interpersonal Attraction,* ed. S. Duck, 249–70. New York: Academic Press, 1972.

Laumann, E.O. Friends of Urban Men: An Assessment of Accuracy in Reporting their Socio-economic Attributes, Mutual Choice, and Attitude Agreement. *Sociometry.* 32:54–69, 1969.

Luckey, E.B. Implications for Marriage Counseling of Self Perceptions and Spouse Receptions. *Journal of Counseling Psychology.* 7:3–9, 1960a.

Luckey, E.B. Marital Satisfaction and Congruent Self-spouse Concepts. *Social Forces.* 39:153–57, 1960b.

Luckey, E.B. Perceptual Congruence of Self and Family Concepts as Related to Marital Interaction. *Sociometry.* 25:234–50, 1962.

Lundy, R.M. Self Perception and Descriptions of Opposite-Sex Sociometric Choices. *Sociometry.* 19:272–77, 1956.

Lundy, R.M. Self Perceptions Regarding Masculinity-Femininity and Description of Same and Opposite-Sex Sociometric Choices. *Sociometry.* 21:238–46, 1958.

Murstein, B.I. Self, Ideal Self Discrepancy, and the Choice of Marital Partners. *Journal of Consulting and Clinical Psychology.* 37:47–52, 1971.

Murstein, B.I. Physical Attractiveness and Marital Choice. *Journal of Personality and Social Psychology.* 22:8–12, 1972a.

Murstein, B.I. Person Perception and Courtship Progress Among Premarital Couples. *Journal of Marriage and the Family.* 34:621–27, 1972b.

Murstein, B.I. *Who will marry whom? Theories and research in marital choice.* New York, NY: Springer Publishing Co., 1976.

Norton, A., and Glick, P. Marital Instability in America: Past, Present, Future. In *Divorce and Separation,* ed. G. Levinger and O.C. Mobs. New York, NY: Basic Books, 1976.

Pam, A., Plutchik, R., and Conte, H. Love: A Psychometric Approach. *Proceedings of the 81st Annual Convention of the American Psychological Association.* 159–60, 1973.

Prather, H. *Notes on Love and Courage.* New York: Doubleday 1977.

Schafer, R., Braito, R., and Bohlen, J. Self Concept and the Reaction of Significant Others: A Comparison of Husbands and Wives. *Sociological Inquiry.* 46:57–66, 1973.

Shantean, J., and Nagy, G. Probability of Acceptance in Dating Choice. *Journal of Personality and Social Psychology.* 37:522–33, 1979.

Stech, S. The Effect of Marital Dissolution on Suicide. *Journal of Marriage and the Family.* 42:83–92, 1980.

Thompson, W., and Nishimura, R. Some Determination of Friendship. *Journal of Personality and Social Psychology.* Vol 10:305–14, 1952.

5

Interpersonal Communication, Sexual Intimacy, Emotional Intimacy, and Interpersonal Relationships

> For communication to have meaning it must have a life. It must transcend "you" and "me" and become "us." If I truly communicate, I see in you a life that is not me and partake of it. And you see and partake of me. In a small way we then grow out of our old selves and become something new. To have this kind of sharing I cannot enter a conversation clutching myself. I must give myself to the relationship, and be willing to be what grows out of it.
>
> Hugh Prather (1977:21).

The Alignment of Sexual and Emotional Intimacy

Central to the successful emergence of a deep interpersonal relationship between individuals of the opposite sex is the problem of affecting alignment between sexual and emotional intimacy. When such alignment is successful the individuals' "you" and "me" become the emergent "us" and the interpersonal relationship is experienced as both personally and relationally satisfying. When such alignment is unsuccessful the individuals' "you" and "me" fail to become the emergent "us," and the attempt to form a deep interpersonal relationship becomes problematic and frequently disatisfying. In either case it is the medium of communication to which the individuals turn in order to establish such alignment or to correct problems of misalignment. Human intuition and considerable research suggest that aligning the relationship between sexual intimacy, emotional intimacy, and the preferred level of interpersonal relationship can be both a complex and problematic process. The *complexity* of the alignment process arises from (1) the substantial differences individuals experience in the meanings they attach to sex, (2) differences between male and female experience in sources, rates, and intensities of sexual arousal and (3) the effect both of these have on the communication of self-concept support. The *problematic* nature of the alignment process arises throughout the life of opposite sex relationships, manifesting itself (1) in premarital and cohabitation patterns, (2) marital conflict and adjustment, and (3) extra-marital and swinging relationships. It will be the purpose of this chapter to explore the complex and problematic nature of effecting alignment between sexual intimacy, emotional intimacy, and the preferred level of interpersonal relationship through interpersonal communication. In so doing we shall first explore the three complexities of the alignment process and then examine their manifestations in premarital and cohabitation patterns, marital conflict and adjustment, and extramarital and swinging relationships.

Aligning Sexual Intimacy and Emotional Intimacy: The Communication Complexities

The impact of sexual behavior on the development of close male-female relationships is not well understood. Only recently have researchers began to explore differences in the personal meaning of sex, differences in the sources, rates and intensities of male-female arousal, and the effect these differences have on the communication of self-concept support, which is the key communication process involved in deepening interpersonal attraction. Let us examine the research findings in each of these areas in order to understand the complexity of the processes involved in aligning sexual and emotional intimacy through communication.

Differences in the Personal Meanings of Sex

In recent years, increased sexual permissiveness has affected interpersonal relationships in four important ways. *First, a greater proportion of unmarried couples* (82%) are engaging in sex prior to marriage (Peplau, Rubin and Hill 1977). *Second, intercourse is occurring at earlier stages in the development of a relationship*, 41% within one month of beginning to date, 82% within six months of meeting (Peplau, Rubin and Hill 1977). *Third, intercourse by married men and women with someone other than their spouses* has increased to the point where 50% of both husbands and wives have had at least one such experience by the age of 40 (Rubenstein 1983). *Fourth, swinging or extra-marital intercourse by both spouses at the same time and in the same place* has increased to the point where 2% of married couples engage in such activities (*Psychology Today* 1983).

While some theorists claim that intercourse with one's own partner or another is an effective means for building emotional intimacy in the primary relationship, others claim that "instant sex" and "extra-marital sex" prevent emotional stability in the primary relationship. Several research findings shed some light on this issue. *First*, there is no *significant difference* in either the *satisfaction rating* or *divorce rate* between couples who engage in coitus prior to marriage and those who do not (Bentler and Newcomb 1980; Peplau, Rubin and Hill 1977). *Second*, there is *no significant difference* in either the *number of couples who marry* or the *number who divorce* based on early (one month), later (six months), or never engaging in premarital intercourse (Bentler and Newcomb 1980; Peplau, Rubin and Hill 1977). *Third*, there is *no significant difference* in *level of marital satisfaction* or *frequency of divorce* between couples who do or do not engage in extra-marital sex (Atwater 1979). *Fourth*, there is a *significant* difference in *levels of marital satisfaction* and *frequency of divorce* between couples who do and those who do not engage in swinging (Danfield and Gordon 1970).

Turner (1970) resolves the controversy regarding the effect of sexual intimacy on emotional intimacy and on the preferred level of interpersonal relationship by arguing that it *depends upon the meaning that people attach to the act of intercourse* and not upon any natural or innate significance of the act itself. Turner's point is that in a society where divorce and sometimes competing meanings are associated with having sex, the participants' own interpretation of such an act becomes the key determinant of its dyadic significance and effect upon the relationship. Thus, one's perceptions, feelings, and understanding are one's reality (Cahn 1983). Studies conducted by Peplau, Rubin, and Hill (1977) and D'Augelli and D'Augelli (1977) support Turner's analysis by revealing three very diverse patterns of relationships based on sexual intimacy, emotional intimacy, and the preferred level of interpersonal relationship.

Sexually Traditional Couples. A minority of 18–20% of their sample adhered to a traditional pattern of sexual behavior. For them intense emotional involvement or love was an insufficient justification for participating in sexual intercourse. Instead they required the more permanent commitment of marriage as well as intense love as a prerequisite for intercourse. For these couples, abstaining from sex was an indication of love and respect, and an indication that the basis for their relationship went deeper than mere physical attraction. For this group the preferred level of interpersonal relationship is marriage. The level of emotional intimacy must be love; then and only then will their level of relationship include intercourse.

Sexually Moderate Couples. A majority, or 52–62% of their sample adhered to a moderate pattern of sexual behavior. For them, sex is permissible if a man or woman love each other, and a long term commitment like marriage is not necessary. Since it takes time for love to develop and grow, "instant sex" is incompatible with this orientation; love or a deep emotional bond is a prerequisite for sex. For this group the level of emotional intimacy must include love; then and only then will the relationship involve intercourse.

Sexually Liberal Couples. A minority, or 20–28% of their sample adhered to a liberal pattern of sexual behavior. For them, sex is an acquaintance device. While this group believes that sex with love is desirable, sex without love is also acceptable. This group is capable of enjoying casual or "recreational" sex as well as seeing intercourse as an expression of emotional sharing and intimacy. For this group "eroticism" may be as important as emotional intimacy for engaging in intercourse. In such instances engaging in sex means nothing regarding their level of emotional intimacy or the preferred level of interpersonal relationship involved in the interaction.

Clearly when two people engage in sexual intercourse and hold the same meaning for that act, little communication difficulty will arise. Both assume the other derives the same meaning from the intercourse. However, when one person holds one meaning for sex and the other holds a quite different meaning, serious communication problems emerge. For example, one person may view intercourse as a certification of love while the other forbids it until after marriage, or one person may view the act as an indication of love and emotional involvement while the other may interpret it simply as an erotic experience which conveys no such commitment. In both of these cases, individual self-concepts as well as the relationship will suffer.

Similarly, two individuals may achieve dyadic consensus on the meaning of sex as either a relational commitment to marriage or an emotional commitment to love and may then choose to engage in intercourse with others outside this primary relationship, employing a recreational or erotic meaning. When members of the dyad have a consensus of the acceptability of these outside relationships, we have the acceptance of swinging or extramarital affairs. When they do not have consensus on such relationships and find out about it, individual self-concepts and the relationship will suffer from what is communicated. Thus, one of the first problems to confront a couple in aligning sexual intimacy, emotional intimacy, and level of preferred relationship is their individual interpretations of the meaning of sex in their primary relationship and in their relationship with others. Without such an understanding individual self-concepts and the dyadic emergence of a successful interpersonal relationship may be impaired.

Differential Sources, Rates, and Intensities of Male and Female Sexual Arousal

All human emotions have both a cognitive and a physiological component (Goldstein, Fink, and Mettee 1972). This is no less true of love and sex than other basic human emotions. The interaction of the cognitive and physiological components determines the overall level of arousal caused by a given emotion (Wincze, Hoon, and Hoon 1973). The overall level of arousal caused by emotional intimacy or love significantly affects the level of self-concept support provided to the other. The level of self-concept support provided to the other significantly affects the level of interpersonal attraction one feels for another person (Carducci, Cozby, and Ward 1978). As we indicated in the last chapter, one's ability to communicate this feeling of attraction or self-concept support is the central factor in the emergence of a mate-relationship. However, substantial male-female differences in the sources, rates, and intensities of sexual arousal significantly complicate the communication problems involved in aligning emotional intimacy, sexual intimacy, and the preferred level of interpersonal relationship.

First, the sources of physiological arousal found in the physical attractiveness and sex appeal of persons of the opposite sex are dependent upon our perception of their respective facial features and body build (MacCorquodale and DeLamater 1979). While there is considerable personal variation in what a person considers physically attractive and sexually appealing in others of the opposite sex, research suggests that we tend to prefer others who we believe are about as physically attractive and sexually appealing as we think we are (Murstein and Christy 1974).

Second, the sources of cognitive arousal found in the physical attractiveness and sex appeal of a person of the opposite sex tend to differ substantially for males and females. Males tend to be attracted by the personal characteristics of the female and tend to idealize and fantasize about past and current love and sexual experiences. Females tend to be attracted by the characteristics of the emergent interpersonal relationship and tend to idealize and fantasize about current and imagined love and sex experiences (McCauley and Swann 1978; Peplau, Rubin and Hill 1977). These differential sources of cognitive arousal may lead to one person's being aroused while the other is not.

Third, the rate of sexual arousal found in males and females tends to differ substantially. Researchers report an average rate of male arousal from intromission to ejaculation of from one to three minutes. Women average eight to ten minutes from intromission to orgasm. This finding has led to the emergence of a rather large literature on the importance of foreplay to help increase female responsiveness and numerous techniques for delaying male orgasm (Butler 1976). These differences may lead to one person's experiencing satisfaction with intercourse while the other does not.

Fourth, the intensity of sexual arousal found in males and females tends to differ substantially in regard to its effect on the accurate perception of another's self-concept. Tests of the effect of sexual arousal on the accurate perception of another's self-concept yield the following results. Males who are high on sexual arousal tests tend to be very inaccurate in understanding the self-concepts of the females they are with. Moderate arousal males are most accurate . . . low arousal males being more accurate than high arousal males but less accurate than moderate arousal males. On the other hand, high arousal females tend to be the most accurate in regard to the self-concept characteristics of their partners, moderate arousal second, and low arousal last. This makes the ideal male-female relationship, in terms of accuracy of self-concept support, a moderate arousal male and a high arousal female. The worst match would be a high arousal male and a low arousal female (Murstein 1972). These differences may lead to couples providing no or inaccurate self-concept support to their partners.

Clearly, when two people are in love and involved in sexual intercourse and, because of differences in the sources, rates, and intensities of arousal, one does not become aroused, does not persistently experience orgasm, or does not provide accurate self-concept support to his or her partner, both their individual self-concepts and their interpersonal relationship may suffer. Several researchers report that communication problems regarding sexual intimacy, emotional intimacy, and relational alignment are reported as the most significant problems confronting male-female relationships in dating, cohabitation, early marriage, and late marriage (Luckey 1960; Landis 1962; Murstein 1972; Christensen and Wallace 1976). They are also among the most difficult problems to resolve. This is particularly true when a male is intensely aroused. In such cases the female may be denied organismic fulfillment and accurate self-concept support, two elements essential to the emergence of successful mate-relationships.

The Effect of Differential Meanings, Sources, Rates, and Intensity of Sexual Arousal on Perceived Self-Concept Support

Successful male-female relationships normally develop by passing through several stages: Those of mate or friend relationships. At each stage of development, differential criteria are applied to determine relational success. For example, relational satisfaction and progress towards marriage are frequent success measures for dating; marital satisfaction and marital adjustment are success measures for the early stages of marriage; and personal growth and relational growth are success measures for the later stages of marriage. At each stage of development, differential antecedents are necessary for scoring high on the various success measures. For example, different variables effect attraction in males and females. For a woman, the perception of love involvement by a man, her satisfaction with a man as an intellectual and stable partner, and her perception of being understood are the powerful variables. For a man, his feeling of being understood, his feeling that a woman is sexually appealing, and his feeling that she is physically attractive are important determinants in successful dating relationships (Murstein 1972). However, as both Murstein (1972) and Schulman (1974) point out, these perceptions are idealized and frequently have little relationship to reality. During early marriage for a man, a woman's clothes-consciousness, his own masculinity, her cheerfulness, and her objectively in seeing her husband as he sees himself are important determinants of marital success. For a woman, a man's thriftiness and emotional support for her, along with dyadic consensus and accuracy in regard to marital roles and affection, are important to successful marital relationships (Bentler and Newcomb 1978; Luckey 1960; Christensen and Wallace 1976). During the later stages of marriage both male and female support and accuracy in regard to the spouses' real and ideal self-concept consensus and accuracy in regard to affection, perception of role delegation, and consensus on mutual friends are important to successful interpersonal relationships (Landis 1962; Luckey 1960; Christian and Wallace 1976).

In short, throughout various stages of successful male-female relationships the communication of perceived self-concept support and affection is important, whether accurately grounded or not. However, as one enters further and further into successful male-female relationships, real-ideal self-concept support and accuracy along with consensus and accuracy regarding affection, role delineation of friendship patterns become central. All of these characteristics require an alignment of emotional intimacy and sexual intimacy as well as consensus and accuracy in regard to individual and relational meanings. A relationship disintegrates where differential meanings exist for sexual intercourse and differential sources, rates, and intensities of arousal are present. Where meanings are mutually agreed to, and differential sources, rates, and intensities of arousal are compensated for, then real and ideal self-concept support and dyadic consensus and accuracy will be achievable through communication. The relationship will then grow and deepen.

Having examined in some detail the complexities involved in aligning communication, emotional intimacy, sexual intimacy, and preferred level of interpersonal relationships, we are now in a position to explore the problems created by these complexities in various types of male-female relationships.

Aligning Sexual Intimacy and Emotional Intimacy in Context: The Communication Problems

The specific problematic character of aligning sexual intimacy, emotional intimacy, and the preferred type of interpersonal relationships manifests itself in pre-marital and cohabitation patterns, marital conflict and adjustment, and in extra-marital and swinging relationships. Let us explore each in turn.

Pre-Marital and Cohabitation Patterns

Traditionally, sexual intimacy and emotional intimacy were regulated by specific male-female role patterns in pre-marital interpersonal relationships. In general, males were expected to initiate sex, while females were expected to set limits on the couple's sexual intimacy based on emotional intimacy (Gagnon and Simon 1973; Safilios-Rothschild 1977; Peplau, Rubin and Hill 1977). For males seeing "how far they could get" served to affirm their masculinity, to acknowledge the females' attractiveness, and to test her meaning for sex. The female demonstrated her popularity and desirability by refusing such requests. Comparisons between 1959, 1972, and 1983 studies of pre-marital sex indicate several changes in this traditional pattern. *First*, today, virtually all men attempt to initiate sexual intercourse (98%) early in a relationship (within the first month). *Second*, now a smaller proportion of women are exercising veto power over intercourse and insisting on a long term commitment (18%). *Third*, presently young people are engaging in pre-marital intercourse at an earlier age then ever before (60% by the age of 19, 83% by the age of 21). *Fourth*, a larger proportion of young people are participating in recreational sex (50%). *Finally*, there has been a rapid rise in the rate of cohabitation from 500,000 to 1,500,000 in the past decade (Peplau, Rubin and Hill 1977; Bell and Coughey 1980; Rubenstein 1983; Jackson 1983). Most of these changes in life-style can be attributed to society's becoming less critical of these behaviors, as long as those involved do not bear children and are economically independent (Glick and Spanier 1980).

The rapid rise in cohabitation-relationships among people of all ages, but in particular the young, the retired, and the divorced, is motivated by several needs:

1. temporary convenience and mutual benefit
2. need for affection
3. trial marriage
4. as an alternative to marriage

(Ridley, Peterman, and Avery 1978)

Again, these motivations differ substantially by sex. Males list the need for positive self-concept support in a heterosexual relationship, the security of a relatively stable intimate relationship and the convenience of sex as the chief motivating factors. Females list the need for emotional attachment and the desire to marry (Macklin 1974, 1978; Arafet and Yorburg 1973; Jackson 1983).

Ridley, Peterman, and Avery (1978) examined the effect of these different motivations on communication, emotional and sexual intimacy, and the preferred level of interpersonal relationships. Four types of cohabitation patterns were discussed: (1) Linus Blanket, (2) Emancipation, (3) Convenience and (4) Testing.

Formation of a *Linus Blanket* type of relationship occurs when an insecure individual seeks a relationship with just about anyone who offers emotional security. The relationship is characterized by a high degree of fragility and seldom leads to the type of communication between partners which creates emotional, sexual, and relational alignment or to the development of the interpersonal communication skills needed to control or to maintain heterosexual relationships. The relationship usually lacks any open communication or successful problem solving. What does take place tends to be ritualized, following traditional lines of male-female behavior providing only opportunities to learn stereotyped sex-role behavior.

The *Emancipation and Convenience* relationships are typical of 75% of the males and females who have had more than one cohabiting experience. These are individuals who report that their longest cohabiting experience lasted less than six months. Characteristic of the *Emancipation* cohabiting relationship is the guilt feeling experienced by one of the cohabitors . . . typically the female. The Catholic female may be a perfect example of a cohabiting participant caught between peer pressure to engage in more sexually liberating behavior and the subsequent feelings of guilt arising from socialization to strict sexual standards established by family and church. The guilt may ultimately cause her to leave the relationship, until internal pressures reassert themselves and she once again becomes involved in cohabiting. This tenuous involvement in the cohabiting relationship does not allow for the alignment of communication, sexual intimacy, emotional intimacy, and preferred levels of interpersonal relationship. However, should the cohabiting experience allow one to work through this value-behavior discrepancy, increased self-knowledge would lead to better future heterosexual relationships.

In the *Convenience* relationship, the male has the luxuries of regular sex and domestic living without the responsibility of a committed relationship. Assuming that the female is designated to perform most or all of the domestic tasks, it is inferred that the male's interpersonal skill level is directly related to the length of time he can keep the female interested in the relationship. The *Convenience* cohabiting situation provides a good opportunity for both a male and a female to learn reciprocity and mutual giving and getting in a relationship. The male may learn about the role behavior associated with the day-to-day aspects of domestic life and at least some exchange and conflict resolution skills. Males typically exhibit a "guarded openness" which serves to prevent communication from achieving the alignment of emotional intimacy, sexual intimacy, and an enduring interpersonal relationship.

In the *Testing* relationship we find well-adjusted individuals who exhibit a higher than average interpersonal skill level upon entrance into the cohabiting environment. The motivation behind forming the relationship has moved well beyond meeting security needs to learning more about themselves and the complexity of intimate relationships. The willingness to get to know one's partner facilitates deeper reciprocal levels of self-disclosure. However, the success in the aligning communication, emotional intimacy, sexual intimacy, and the preferred level of interpersonal relationship depends upon the successful maintenance of each individual's self-identity while constructing a commitment to an enduring interpersonal relationship. There is the possibility that the partners may feel overinvolved and dependent on the relationship, with an accompanying sense of loss of individual identity which in turn may lead to a termination of the *Testing* relationship.

In short, because of substantial motivational differences in entering into cohabitation, most cohabitants are not inclined to develop the communication patterns necessary to overcome differences in the meaning of sex, differences in male-female sources, rates, and intensities of arousal, and the effect of those differences upon the accuracy of self-concept support and relational consensus. It is therefore not surprising that cohabitation is less effective than traditional dating patterns in developing enduring male-female relationship, although this generalization does not hold for Testing cohabitation patterns (Jackson 1983; Rank 1981). In this later instance cohabitation is an important intermediate step in the formation of mate-relationships. In all other cases cohabitors are more likely than traditional daters or married couples to indicate that they have become upset by feelings of overinvolvement in a relationship and upset by feelings that their partners do not love them as much as they once did (Budd 1977).

Marital Conflict and Adjustment

Marriage offers almost the ideal context within which to align communication, emotional intimacy, sexual intimacy, and the preferred level of interpersonal relationship. In marriage an ideal context is created for frequent and open communication. In marriage both parties normally achieve consensus on the appropriate level of emotional involvement . . . love. In marriage even the most traditional of individuals along with the most liberal believe it to be the appropriate level of interpersonal relationship . . . mateship. While all of this may be true, several significant findings suggest that not all is well with alignment in such situations.

First, several studies demonstrate that effective communication is strongly associated with the quality of marital relationships, dyadic satisfaction, affectional expression, cohesion, consensus, and global measures of marital satisfaction and adjustment (Honeycutt, Wilson and Parker 1982). *Second*, research suggests that marital partners seek love, companionship, romance, financial security, and sex from their relationship (Rubenstein 1983). *Third*, love consists of three primary elements: friendship, devotion, and intellectual compatibility (Rubenstein 1983). *Fourth*, research reveals that 40% of married women and 28% of married men report a lack of love and desire for sex in their relationship (Rubenstein 1983). *Fifth*, research indicates that in general the longer a couple have been married the more ritualized and unsatisfying their communication, emotional intimacy, and sexual intimacy become (*Newsweek* 1981). *Sixth*, fully one-third of all married woman believe their marriage may end in divorce (Rubenstein 1983).

Equally disconcerting is a recent study by Swenson, Eskew, and Kohlhepp (1981) which indicates a steady decline in both love and conflict for married couples over the family life cycle. (See chart on p.77).

In an attempt to locate communication behaviors which might serve to counter these disturbing trends, Navran (1967) explored when and how interpersonal communication can contribute to relational growth and satisfaction rather than disintegration and dissatisfaction in marriage. He found a strong relationship ($r = .91$) between the following communication behavior and relational growth:

- much more frequently talk over pleasant things that happen during the day.

- feel more frequently understood by their spouses; i.e., their messages are getting across.

- discuss things which are shared interests.

- are less likely to break communication or inhibit it by pouting.

- more often will talk with each other about personal problems.

- make more frequent use of words which have a private meaning for them.

- generally talk most things over together.

- are more sensitive to each other's feelings and make adjustments to take these into account when they speak.

- are more free to discuss intimate issues without restraint or embarrassment.

- are more able to tell what kind of day their spouses have had without asking.

- communicate non-verbally to a greater degree, via the exchange of glances.

From these items of communication behavior, Navran concluded that happily married couples differ from unhappily married couples in that they:

1) talk more to each other.
2) convey the feeling that they understand what is being said to them.
3) have a wider range of subjects available to them.

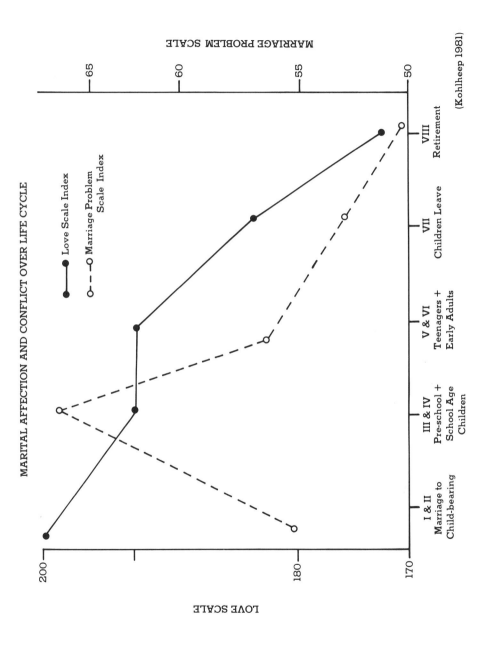

MARITAL AFFECTION AND CONFLICT OVER LIFE CYCLE

MARRIAGE PROBLEM SCALE

LOVE SCALE

● Love Scale Index
○ Marriage Problem
   Scale Index

I & II
Marriage to
Child-bearing

III & IV
Pre-school +
School Age
Children

V & VI
Teenagers +
Early Adults

VII
Children Leave

VIII
Retirement

(Kohlheep 1981)

4) preserve communication channels and keep them open.
5) show more sensitivity to each other's feelings.
6) personalize their language symbols.
7) make more use of supplementary non-verbal techniques of communication.

Similarly, several studies report a strong relationship between these types of communication behaviors and marital adjustment (r = .80) and the absence of these behaviors with marital conflict (r = .71) (Margolin 1978). In addition, the best predictors of relational discord in marriage are still (1) lack of consensus between spouses on the desired levels of affection, love, and sex and (2) weak or inaccurate self-concept support (Christensen and Wallace 1976; Luckey 1960). Landis (1962) reports on the length of time it takes couples to achieve relational consensus in various marital coordination areas such as spending, friends, marital roles, and affection. The most problematic area for married couples is the area of affection . . . in particular, sex. Landis reports that 53% of marital couples he surveyed achieved consensus on the level of sexual intimacy prior to marriage, another 13% within the first year, and another 10% within two years for a total of 76%. However, 24% reported never achieving such a consensus, thus becoming prime prospects for relational failure. Furthermore, for the 76% who did achieve consensus at one point in time, there is danger that sexual intimacy will become ritualized, thus preventing relational growth and creating an environment for relational boredom.

Conflict over emotional intimacy and sexual intimacy are common in marital relationships and may lead to relational disintegration (Horowitz 1979). This is particularly true when the couple lacks the communication skills necessary to resolve such conflicts (Rim 1979). Conflicts of this type are best resolved by building a clear agenda of problems and then by negotiating behavioral changes aimed at correcting the problems (Gottman 1979). This may involve educating one or more of the individuals involved regarding the diversities in meaning, sources, rates, and intensities of arousal and their effect on self-concept support in regard to sex.

Marital interaction offers an ideal opportunity for couples to align communication, emotional intimacy, sexual intimacy, and the preferred level of interpersonal relationships. With proper communication and conflict resolution skills, relational satisfaction and marital adjustment can be achieved. However, once alignment is achieved couples must be careful to seek relational growth and avoid ritualized behavior or their marriage may become boring and lead to marital discord or even divorce.

Extra-Marital Sex and Swinging

Marital boredom and discord can lead to a search for emotional and/or sexual intimacy outside the marital relationship. Extra-marital sex and swinging are frequently associated with male and female perceptions of unsatisfying sexual intimacy in marriage. Extra-marital sex is one spouse's attempt to seek sexual fulfillment outside the marital relationship without jeopardizing the emotional intimacy of marriage; swinging occurs when both spouses seek more open extra-marital sexual intimacy, and do this with full knowledge of one another's actions and in close proximity to one another.

Recent studies indicate that by age 40 50% of all married couples have participated in one or more extra-marital affairs (Rubenstein 1983). This represents a significant rise in female extra-marital sexual activity. Perhaps the most extensive and careful analysis of female extra-marital sex (EMS) was conducted by Atwater in 1974–75. A careful examination of her results is insightful regarding the motivation, process, and effects of extra-marital affairs. She interviewed in depth 40 women who had participated in EMS. They varied in age from 23 to 59 years and in education from high school to graduate degrees. Occupationally, about one-third were homemakers, one-third held full time clerical jobs, and one-third were in managerial or professional positions. Thirty-eight percent had EMS with only one partner, the remainder had multiple involvements. Three women were involved in open marriages and told their husbands; the others did not. Atwater (1979) investigated the process of EMS involvement by dividing it into four stages: pre-involvement, involvement, the experiences of EMS, and post-experience effects.

Pre-involvement variables. Atwater found that 80% of the women had had premarital sex with their husbands and 40% of these had premarital experiences with at least one other man. For the overwhelming majority (95%), there was no concern or thought of becoming involved in EMS at the time of marriage. In 100% of the cases these women became aware of the opportunity to participate in EMS when approached and repeatedly asked to do so by a man. About 50% of the women knew some other women who had been involved in EMS. Most were peers, but 15% were parents or other relatives. About 55% of the women recall specific conversations with others about EMS before their involvement and half of these were reported as a significant factor in their decision. Approximately one-fourth discussed the possibility of EMS with their husbands. Three-quarters of the women thought about becoming involved before doing so. The length of time averaged one month.

Involvement variables. Only four of 40 women reported being in "love" with the other man at the time they became involved in EMS. Not only were the others not involved, they did not become so even after repeated interactions with the same man. The woman reported that rarely was the "person" more important than the "situation" in getting involved. In about 50% of the cases unsatisfactory marriages were part of the situational motivation. In 100% of the cases the males initiated the action which precipitated sexual involvement.

Experiences of EMS. First, in all cases the basic reaction was favorable, ranging from simple enjoyment to extreme pleasure. A second theme running through the reactions was a sense of learning, self-recognition, and self-discovery. Only about 25% reported emotional involvement as a reaction to their experiences.

Post-Experience variables. About 75% of the women justified their involvement by assuming responsibility for their actions and claiming they were self-fulfilling.

About 25% denied responsibility for their actions . . . "it just happened." One-half of these women felt guilty; the others did not. All enjoyed the experience. Approximately 63% established patterns of repeating EMS with other partners after the relationship with their first partner ended. One-half of these women engaged in multiple involvements at the same time. Of the remainder who had only one involvement, 60% were still on-going at the time of the interview. About 89% of the women said they would have additional EMS in the future, while the remainder did not know if they would go beyond their present involvement.

Clearly, extra-marital sex is not an emotionally intimate experience. Rather, it tends to be an intentional, planned, situationally motivated process for gaining personal and sexual satisfaction outside one's primary interpersonal relationship. As such, EMS does not lead to an alignment of emotional intimacy and sexual intimacy. It contributes to the development of a recreational meaning for sex. It may or may not prepare one to deal with male and female differences in the sources, rates, and intensities of arousal as well as the effects these have on accurately communicating self-concept support. It does appear to help one's personal fulfillment and could contribute to self-concept understanding. However, it also runs the risk of destroying the trust in one's primary relationship if discovered by the spouse.

On a regular basis, swinging is engaged in by less than 2% of the marital population (Murstein 1978). There are two basic kinds of swingers, groups and couples. Most couples become swingers because the husband persuades the wife to do so (Henshel 1973). Most wives react to the suggestion with shock and fear that something is wrong with their marriage. Two reasons tend to motivate men to make such a suggestion . . . first, to use the wife to gain access to other women and second, to encourage the wife to develop her own sexual technique (Varni 1972). Women swingers often become bisexual—65% in one sample (Murstein 1978). Where couples who swing develop friendships, their sexual interactions often decrease or terminate. Most swingers eventually "drop out" or stop swinging. Danfield and Gordon (1970) studied the reasons swingers provide for dropping out (see statistics below).

Problems	No. of Couples	%
Jealousy	109	23
Guilt	68	14
Threatening Marriage	68	14
Emotional Attachment with other partner	53	11
Boredom	49	11
Disappointment	33	7
Divorce	29	7
Wife can't take it	29	7
Impotency husband	14	3
Fear of Discovery	15	3
	467	100%

Swinging, like extra-marital sex, appears not to contribute to the alignment between emotional intimacy and sexual intimacy. Instead it has quite an adverse effect upon marital relationships. It fails to enhance the communication of self-concept support and tends to confuse the various meanings of sex between couples. In short, it is destructive of marital relationships.

We began this chapter by drawing attention to the complexities and problems involved in aligning communication, emotional intimacy, sexual intimacy, and the preferred level of interpersonal relationship. We noted communication complexities resulting from: (1) the differential meaning of sex, (2) different sources, rates, and intensity of male and female arousal, and (3) the effect of these on communicating self-concept support and achieving relational consensus. An examination of the relational contexts for alignment . . . namely premarital sex and cohabitation patterns, marital conflict and adjustment, and extra-marital sex and swinging patterns . . . revealed several problems. First, premarital sex and cohabitation patterns tended not to allow for alignment, because of the different motivation of the participants in the process. The one exception to this pattern was the *Testing* cohabitation pattern, which did assist the alignment process. Second, while marriage in general and marital conflict and adjustment in particular did assist in alignment for a majority of participants, alignment in time gives way to ritualization and boredom at another time if not carefully monitored. Third, extra-marital sex and swinging did not contribute significantly to alignment and could become very destructive to the mate-relationship. The alignment of communication, emotional intimacy, sexual intimacy, and interpersonal relationship continues to be a serious problem for interpersonal communication and the maintenance of enduring inter-personal relationships.

Propositions

1. Alignment of sexual and emotional intimacy is central to the emergence of a deep interpersonal relationship.
2. When sexual and emotional intimacy are aligned, the individuals' "you" and "me" become the emergent "us" in a satisfying interpersonal relationship.
3. To establish alignment or to correct misalignment in interpersonal relationships, individuals turn to the medium of communication.
4. Complexity in alignment of relationships is due to differences in meanings attached to sex, to differences in sources, rates and intensities of sexual arousal, and to the difference effects these variable meanings and experiences have on the communication of self-concept support.
5. Problems in alignment manifest themselves in three pre-marital patterns, in marital conflict and adjustment, and in extra-marital and swinging relationships.

6. Increased sexual permissiveness has affected interpersonal relationships so that a greater proportion of unmarried couples engage in sex prior to marriage, intercourse occurs at earlier stages in the development of a relationship, intercourse by married men and women with a non-spouse has increased, and swinging, or extra-marital intercourse by both spouses at the same time and in the same place, has increased.

7. In American society, diverse and competing meanings are associated with intercourse and the participants' own interpretations of the act become the key determinants of its significance and its effect upon the relationship.

8. Sexually traditional couples prefer abstinence from sex until that level of emotional intimacy is legitimatized in marriage.

9. Sexually moderate couples engage in sex without the bond of marriage if the man and woman "love each other."

10. Sexually liberal couples believe sex with love is desirable, but not mandatory for enjoyment; these couples are capable of enjoying casual or "recreational" sex as well as of seeing intercourse as an expression of emotional sharing and intimacy.

11. Sources of physiological arousal found in physical attractiveness and sex appeal are dependent upon our perception of facial features and body build; we tend to prefer others we believe are about as physically attractive and sexually appealing as we think we are.

12. Males tend to be attracted by personal characteristics of the female and tend to idealize and fantasize about past and current love and sexual experiences; females tend to be attracted by the characteristics of the emergent interpersonal relationship and tend to idealize and fantasize about current and imagined love and sex experiences.

13. Male and female sexual arousal rates differ considerably, with male arousal occuring significantly sooner; this difference may lead to loss of satisfaction between partners.

14. Intensity of sexual arousal differs in regard to accurate perception of another's self-concept, with moderate-arousal males and high-arousal females most accurate in regard to the self-concept characteristics of their partners.

15. At each stage of development of an intimate relationship, differential antecedents are necessary for high scoring on success measures.

16. Throughout various stages of successful male-female relationships the communication of perceived self-concept is important, whether or not accurately grounded.

17. Pre-marital and cohabitation patterns have changed from a pattern in which males initiated sex and females set limits on a couple's sexual intimacy based on emotional intimacy, to patterns in which nearly all men attempt to initiate sexual intercourse early in a relationship: women are less likely to veto intercourse and insist on a long-term commitment, young people are engaging in intercourse at an earlier age and are participating in recreational sex, and many more couples are cohabitating prior to marriage.

18. Premarital sex and cohabitation patterns tend to not allow for alignment due to difference in the motivation of the participants in the process, with the one exception of the *Testing* cohabitation pattern, which did assist the alignment process.

19. Effective communication is strongly associated with the quality of marital relationship, dyadic satisfaction, affectional expression, and other global measures; however, large percentages of married men and women report lack of love and sexual desire in their relationship, with those married longest reporting more ritualized and unsatisfying communication and intimacy.

20. Married couples talk more to each other, convey feelings of mutual understanding, have a wider range of subjects, keep communication channels open, and generally make more use of personalized and non-verbal techniques of communication.

21. Conflict over emotional and sexual intimacy in marriage may lead to relational disintegration, and this conflict may be best resolved by building a clear agenda of problems and by negotiating behavioral changes aimed at correcting the problem.

22. Extra-marital sex tends to be an intentional, planned, and situationally motivated process for gaining personal and sexual satisfaction outside one's primary interpersonal relationship, and as such it does not lead to an alignment of emotional and sexual intimacy.

23. Swinging, like extra-marital sex, does not contribute to alignment between emotional and sexual intimacy but is destructive to the interpersonal relationship.

References

Arafet, I., and Yorburg, B. On Living Together Without Marriage. *Journal of Sex Research.* 9, No. 2:97–106, 1973.

Atwater, L. Getting Involved. *Alternative Life Styles.* 2, No. 1:33–68, 1979.

Bell, R., and Coughey, K. Premarital Sexual Experience Among College Females, 1958, 1968, and 1978. *Family Relations.* 29:353–57, 1980.

Bentler, P., and Newcomb, M. Longitudinal Study of Marital Success and Failure. *Journal of Consulting and Clinical Psychology.* 6, No. 5:1053–70, 1980.

Budd, L. Problems, Disclosures and Commitment of Cohabiting and Married Couples. *Dissertation Abstract International.* 37:6789–90, 1977.

Butler, C. New Data about Female Sexual Response. *Journal of Sex and Marital Therapy.* 2, (1):36–46, 1976.

Cahn, D., Relative Importance of Perceived Understanding in Initial Interaction and Development of Interpersonal Relationships. *Psychological Reports.* 52:923–29, 1983.

Carducci, B., Cozby, P., and Ward, C. Sexual Arousal and Interpersonal Evaluations. *Journal of Experimental Social Psychology.* 14:449–57, 1978.

Christensen, L., and Wallace, L. Perceptual Accuracy as a Variable in Marital Adjustment. *Journal of Sex and Marital Therapy*. 2, 2:130–35, 1976.

Danfield, D., and Gordon, M. The Sociology of Mate Swapping or the Family that Swings Together Clings Together. *Journal of Sex Research*. 6:85–100, 1970.

D'Augelli, J., and D'Augelli A. Moral Reasoning and Permarital Sexual Behavior Toward Reasoning About Relationships. *Journal of Social Issues*. 33, 2:46–66, 1977.

Gagnon, J., and Simon, W. *Sexual Conduct: The Social Sources of Human Sexuality*. Chicago, IL: Aldine, 1973.

Glick, P., and Spainer, G. Married and Unmarried Cohabitation in the United States. *Journal of Marriage and the Family*. 42:19–30, 1980.

Goldstein, D., Fink, D., and Mettee, D. Cognition of Arousal and Actual Arousal as Determinants of Emotion. *Journal of Personality and Social Psychology*. 21:41–51, 1972.

Gottman, J. *Marital Interaction: Experimental Investigations*. Academic Press, N.Y.:1979.

Henshel, A.M. Swinging: A Study of Decision Making in Marriage. *American Journal of Sociology*. 78, 4:885–91, 1973.

Honeycutt, J., Wilson, C., and Parker C. Effects of Sex and Degrees of Happiness on Perceived Styles of Communicating In and Out of The Marital Relationship. *Journal of Marriage and the Family*. 44:395–406, 1982.

Horowitz, L. On the Cognitive Structure of Interpersonal Problems Treated in Psychotherapy. *Journal of Consulting and Clinical Psychology*. 47, 3:5–15, 1979.

Jackson, P. On Living Together Unmarried. *Journal of Family Issues*. 4, 5:35–59, 1983.

Landis, J. "Length of Time Required to Achieve Adjustment in Marriage", *American Sociological Review*. 672–681, 1962.

Luckey, E. Marital Satisfaction and Congruent Self-Spouse Concepts. *Social Forces*. 39:153–57, 1960.

MacCorquodale, P., and DeLamater, J., Self-Image and Premarital Sexuality. *Journal of Marriage and the Family*. 41:327–39, 1979.

Macklin, E. Cohabitation In College: Going Very Steady. *Psychology Today*. 8 (6):53–59, 1974.

Macklin, E. Nonmarital Heterosexual Cohabitation: A Review of the Recent Literature. *Marriage and Family Review*. 1–12, 1978.

Margolin, G. A Multilevel Approach to the Assessment of Communication Positiveness in Distressed Marital Couples. *American Journal of Family Therapy*. 6 (1):81–89, 1978.

McCauley, C., and Swann, C. Male-Female Differences in Sexual Fantasy. *Journal of Research in Personality*. 12:76–86, 1978.

Murstein, B. Swinging in Bernard Murstein, (ed). *Exploring Intimate Life Styles*, Springer, N.Y., 1978.

Murstein, B. *Who Will Marry Whom?* New York: Springer, 1976.

Murstein, B., and Christy, P. Physical Attractiveness and Marriage Adjustment in Middle Aged Couples. University of Connecticut, CT: Unpublished paper, 1974.

Navran, L. Communication and Adjustment in Marriage. *Family Process*. 6:173–84, 1967.

Newsweek, 73–76, July 13, 1981.

Peplau, L., Rubin, Z., and Hill C. Sexual Intimacy in Dating Relationships. *Journal of Social Issues*. 33 (2):80–109, 1977.

Prather, H. *Notes on Love and Courage*. New York, NY: Doubleday 1977.

Rank, M. The Transition To Marriage. *Alternative Life Styles*. 14 (4):487–506, 1981.

Ridley, C., Peterman, D., and Avery, A. Cohabitation: Does It Make For A Better Marriage. *The Family Coordinator*. 29:129–36, 1978.

Rim, Y. Personality and Means of Influence in Marriage. *Human Relations*. 32, 10:871–75, 1979.

Rubenstein, C. The Modern Art of Courtly Love. *Psychology Today*. 42–49, July 1983.

Safilios-Rothschild, C. *Love, Sex and Sex Roles*. Englewood Cliffs, NJ: Prentice Hall, 1977.

Schulman, M. Idealization in Engaged Couples. *Journal of Marriage and the Family*. 139–46, 1974.

Swensen, C., Eskew, R., and Kohlhepp, K. Stages of Family Life Cycle, Ego Development and the Marital Relationship. *Journal of Marriage and the Family*. 43:84–53, 1981.

Turner, R.H. *Family Interaction*. New York, NY: Wiley, 1970.

Varni, C. An Exploratory Study of Spouse-Swapping. *Pacific Sociological Review*. 507–622, 1972.

Wincze, J., Hoon, P., and Hoon, E. Sexual Arousal in Women: A comparison of Cognitive and Physiological Responses by Continuous Measurement. *Archives of Sexual Behavior*. 6(2):121–33, 1977.

6

Interpersonal Communication and the Reassessment of Relationships

> Today at lunch Joe told me that he and Ann had decided to get married in three weeks. "That makes the engagement as long as the courtship." I found myself liking the absurd symmetry of that as much as Joe did. What I didn't like was what he said next: "I've never met anyone quite like her; she has everything I could possibly want." He was filling in all the blanks. I have seen so many marriages and even friendships end when the inevitable realization comes that something was left out of the other person.
>
> Hugh Prather (1977:15).

Relational Stress and Satisfaction

It is an important and yet commonplace observation that until they become problematic we as individuals tend to take our interpersonal relationships for granted. The *importance* of such relationships stems from the fact that in the latter half of the twentieth century most Americans report that the quality of their life is determined not by economic or health considerations but rather by the number and quality of their interpersonal relationships (Campbell 1980). Individuals who have many close friends and a happy marriage tend to report less physical and psychological illness, live longer, and report greater satisfaction with life than those with fewer friends and troubled marriages (Duck 1981). The *commonplaceness* of friends and mate-relationships in our society is deceptive in that it masks the complexities involved in forming and maintaining such interpersonal relationships. Since nearly everyone we know has friends and many also have mates, we forget how difficult it is to establish and to maintain such relationships and how much loneliness and stress are involved when they end.

Researchers tell us that the attempt to *initiate* interpersonal relationships is stressful (Bryant and Trower 1974). They note that 54% of the individuals we approach as friends (Laumann 1969) and 92% of the individuals we approach as mates (Murstein 1976) will decline our offers to form such intimate relationships. Such rejections are associated with extreme feelings of anxiety, the questioning of one's personal worth, and high stress. Researchers tell us that the attempt to *maintain* interpersonal relationships when they are made problematic is stressful

(Bryant and Trower 1974). They note that in any intimate relationship times will arise when misunderstandings take place, disruptions occur, or conflicts emerge to threaten the normal flow of interaction and, at times, the relationship itself. Such descriptions are associated with feelings of confusion, anger, and questioning of oneself and others that create high stress (Dryden 1981). Finally, researchers tell us that the *disintegration* of interpersonal relationships creates loneliness (Perlman and Peplau 1981), family disorders (Orford and O'Reilly 1981), and depression (Dryden 1981). They tell us that 40% of our romantic relationships (Hill, Rubin and Peplau 1976) and 50% of our marriages will end within two to five years after they are established. Such terminations of close relationships are associated with feelings of loneliness, self-doubt, and at times serious psychological, social, and economic deprivation (Trower 1981; Newcomb and Bentler 1981; Duck 1981).

Since success in interpersonal relationships is so comforting and satisfying, and problems in interpersonal relationships so stressful and dissatisfying, the topic of relational assessment is one that must be approached with care and understanding. A working knowledge of how to productively assess our most intimate relationships and how to preserve and repair them when problems arise can be among the most important and useful tools of interpersonal communication. The reasons for relational reassessment are legion: inattention, boredom, breakdown, excitement, happiness, growth, and disintegration, to name but a few. While the causes of relational reassessment are numerous, the results tend to be somewhat more limited, involving (1) continuation, (2) repair, (3) renegotiation and (4) disengagement. It will be the purpose of this chapter to explore the criteria involved in relational reassessment and the role of interpersonal communication in each of the four instances listed above. Prior to this analysis, we must locate the appropriate criteria involved in assessing interpersonal relationships by examining what constitutes a quality communication environment, one in which interpersonal relationships can flourish.

A Quality Communication Environment

A quality communication environment, according to Montgomery (1981), is one which provides an opportunity for both individual and relational growth. Individual and relational development in turn are associated with feelings of self-worth and relational satisfaction. Researchers tell us that self-worth and relational satisfaction are the product of (1) perceived positive self-concept support, (2) self-concept accuracy, and (3) interaction management skills.

Positive self-concept support. In Chapter One we explored how and why the recognition of individual self-concepts was a prerequisite for significant cooperation from others. In Chapter Two we explored the symbolic structure, function, and scope of individual self-concepts, and how they came into being and were tested in interaction with others. The role positive self-concept support plays in the development of individual self-concepts and the initiation and maintenance of friend and mate-relationships were explored in Chapters Three and Four. Positive self-concept support was demonstrated to be an important factor, if not the most important factor, in self-concept and relational development and in an individual's feelings of self-worth and relational satisfaction. Watzlawick, Bevin, and Jackson (1967) examined three communication responses one can provide to any individual's presentation of self and/or attempt to initiate a relationship . . . confirmation, rejection, and disconfirmation. *Confirmation* responses provide feedback to others that one accepts their presentation of self or proposed relationship. Such positive self-concept support communicates an endorsement of the other's self or proposed relationship. *Rejection* responses provide feedback to others that one understands the other's presentation of self and/or the proposed relationship, but rejects it. *Disconfirmation* responses provide feedback to others that one refuses to recognize the reality of the other's presentation of self and/or proposed relationship. According to these authors a confirming response communicates that "you are right," a rejection that "you are wrong," and a disconfirmation that "you do not exist." *A quality communication environment for the development of self-worth and relational satisfaction must contain a preponderance of positive self-concept support or confirmation responses from others* (Cissna 1975; Clark 1973; Larson 1965). Any environment which contains a preponderance of rejection responses or disconfirmation responses will lead to a disintegration of self and/or relationship and of one's feelings of personal worth and relational satisfaction (Gottman, Markman and Notarius 1977; Baxter 1979).

Self-concept accuracy. Each of us has had one or both of the following experiences. First, someone we value highly communicates to us that they expect us to do something we know we cannot do and know we will let them down when we fail. Second, we select a present for someone we value highly and later discover that our present was not well received because we had misjudged what that person liked. The lesson in both cases is the same and is well documented in the research literature. Self-concept accuracy is essential to predicting the effect of our behavior on others (Christensen and Wallace 1976), to achieving an empathic understanding of others (Bernstein and Davis 1982), to achieving relational adjustment (Frank and Kupfer 1976), and to achieving personal and relational happiness (Corsini 1956). When we misjudge others or they misjudge us, both parties will be disappointed. At the center of our feelings of personal worth and relational satisfaction is our capacity both to understand others and to pattern others' expectations for us in an accurate and realistic manner so that neither party finds our behaviors disappointing or rejects or disconfirms our actions. *Disappointment* leads to self-concept and relational disintegration, *self-concept accuracy* leads to self-concept and relational growth. Self-concept accuracy is the responsibility of both individuals involved in an interaction. The skills involved are the listening, cueing, and negotiating skills discussed in Chapter Two. Each interactant has the responsibility of attempting to accurately perceive the other and of helping the other to be accurately perceptive in turn.

Interactional management skills. In one sense interactional management skills refer to all the material covered up to this point in this book. Certainly self-concept development, presentation, and validation skills are involved as well as those skills involved in utilizing the friendship and mate formation processes. However, all of these cueing, listening, and negotiation skills are employed in new and creative ways when one seeks to continue, repair, renegotiate, or disengage from a relationship. In the remaining subsections of this chapter we will explore instances of each of these types of relational reassessment and the specific interactional management skills involved. In so doing, we hope to indicate how to develop one's communicative competence or interactional management skills.

Positive self-concept support, self-concept accuracy and interactional management skills are criteria for a quality communication environment for interpersonal relationships. Without positive self-concept support an individual's attempts to validate his or her self-concept and to initiate friend–and mate-relationships will fail. Without self-concept accuracy an individual and those who interact with him or her will misjudge and disappoint others, leading to relational termination. Finally, without interactional management skills every interactional error has the potential to harm either or both of the selves and the relationship. These then are criteria by which we may reassess our interpersonal communication environment and the interpersonal relationships that exist in it, in order to determine whether such relationships warrant continuation, repair, renegotiation, or disengagement.

The Continuation of a Relationship

This day has been magical. I have been with three friends, one at a time, and I have learned that friends can transform you. The first held me up so I could see. I was able to distinguish the points where things touch, and where they divide, the essential forms coming at me from the future, new elements and consummations, and the old principles that must not be neglected. I could name them all. They spilled from my mouth. He was delighted with my concepts. He didn't seem to realize that he was the one who had given me the vision. My second friend made me gentle and earnest. She needed to talk, and so we talked for a long time. She thanked me for my concern as I was leaving, but she wouldn't have recognized me if I had been any other way. The third friend turned me into a clown, a gesturer, a creator of quips. I hadn't known my life was filled with so much absurdity. He laughed and laughed because he had made me so funny. My friends don't know what they have done today. It's nothing to them: they do it so often. I expect I must also cause a change in them. And so we . . . each a separate we . . . exist only in each other's presence. That is something precious, enough so not to walk away from easily.

(Prather 1977: 42)

Nothing is more exciting or personally rewarding than to reflect upon our interpersonal relationship with friends, and to grasp how and why our feelings of self-worth and relational satisfaction follow from the interactional characteristics of the people involved. Continuing such a relationship involves the use of such interactional management skills as appropriative and synesic role-taking in order to indicate to others and to perceive in others changes in individual self-concepts and increased reciprocal positive self-concept support and self-concept accuracy in order to deepen the relationship. An understanding of such relationships provides us with knowledge of both who we are and what we can become with the help of others. A working knowledge of the central issues involved in such an environment can be developed through an examination of the following Twenty Question Statement Tests of the real self-concept characteristics of several persons involved in friend relationships.

First, note that Bill and all his friends are intelligent, talkative, supportive, good listeners and thoughtful. These characteristics contribute to strong interpersonal attraction in a friend-relationship by providing a common set of self-concept qualities to admire, while creating supportive, accurate, and intense interaction. Second, note that Bill and Don are in addition, theoretic, exciting, and honest, complementing one specific aspect of each other's self-concept and encouraging its development and growth. Third, note that Bill and Bob are hard working, complementing that specific aspect of each other's self-concept development. Finally, note that Bill and Joe are funny, jokers, and playful, complementing that specific aspect of each other's self-concept. In short, Bill has a group of friends that all have some positive self-concept characteristics in common, providing for group self-concept support, self-concept accuracy, and interactional management skills. In addition each has some characteristics that are positive but different from the common core, thus allowing each a unique contribution to Bill's self-

Table 8

Real Self-Concepts for Bill, Don,
Bob and Joe—A Group of Friends

Bill	Don	Bob	Joe
1. Theoretic	Thoughtful	Honest	Joker
2. Intelligent	Good Listener	Helpful	Happy
3. Talkative	Smart	Good Listener	Talkative
4. Supportive	Talkative	Smart	Caring
5. Good Listener	Intelligent	Hard Working	Quick
6. Funny	Happy	Supportive	Intelligent
7. Hard Working	Excitable	Understanding	Good Listener
8. Exciting	Honest	Happy	Thoughtful
9. Honest	Supportive	Talkative	Supportive
10. Thoughtful	Theoretic	Thoughtful	Playful

concept and relational development. Taken as a group they provide Bill with a quality communication environment for his interpersonal relationships, creating self-concept and relational growth. These relationships when assessed should obviously be continued and deepened.

The Repair of a Relationship

> We talked again last night. What he doesn't seem to realize is that if he isn't loyal to someone, if there isn't someone his guts will simply not allow him to manipulate, then his life is going to be a succession of discovered deceits. His treacheries are so reasonable that he thinks any understanding friend would forgive him. But he will not be forgiven. Time and again he will be abandoned. Loyalty is not reasonable. It is the easiest sentiment of all to argue against. If we have a friend we sometimes act against our own best interests. A time may come when we appear quite self-destructive because we have this friend and there is something we must do for him. There are worse things than losing money, losing position, even than losing life; and if we have a friend we can sense that. But what words could I use that would reach inside him and trigger such a feeling? I couldn't explain why anyone would want to be that way, when he knows that he has the alternative of acting rationally and living an orderly life.

(Prather 1977: 65)

Occasionally, we have a friend who makes the error of overstepping the boundaries of friendship by performing, either once or repeatedly, an act that threatens to undermine the relationship. Most often that act is done without an understanding of the effect it will have on the relationship. When that happens three courses of action are open to us: (1) ignore the act and treat it as an accident, (2) break off the relationship by withdrawing, or (3) confront the friend by indicating the problem and its effect and ask for an *account*. If the friend accurately perceives the violation of expectation and its effect and wants to preserve the relationship, then an account should be forthcoming aimed at re-aligning the relationship. Such realignment strategies are essential for interactional management when relationships become problematic. Re-alignment strategies are socially acceptable vocabularies which effect interpersonal alignment in two ways. *First*, "they sustain the flow of joint action by bringing individuals back into line with one another in problematic circumstances." *Second*, "they sustain a relationship between ongoing conduct and culture in the face of a recognized failure of conduct to live up to the cultural established expectation" (Stokes and Hewitt 1976: 844). While there are a variety of re-alignment strategies it is Scott and Lyman's (1968) use of *accounts* which seems most useful here. An account is a particular type of utterance which attempts to bridge the gap between unanticipated behavior and another's expectations. It is the creation of utterances to explain bad, wrong, inept, or unwelcome behavior.

Accounts are of four major types: (1) excuses, (2) justifications, (3) concessions, and (4) refusals. *Excuses* are accounts in which one admits the act in question is bad, wrong, or inappropriate, but denies full responsibility for the act. "I did say that when I should not have, but the policeman made me." *Justifications* are accounts in which one accepts responsibility for the act in question, but denies the pejorative quality associated with it. "I did say that, but it didn't hurt anyone." *Concessions* are accounts in which one admits responsibility for an act and offers restitution or compensation. "I did say that, but I am very sorry. Please take these flowers as atonement for my error." *Refusals* are accounts in which one denies or evades the negative qualities of the deed. "I did say that and it will make you a better person." Excuses, justifications, concessions, and refusals are all socially acceptable vocabularies for neutralizing an act or its consequences when one or both are called into question. In this way, accounts re-align individual identities and relationships when they are called into question. Such a set of interactional management skills is essential to a quality communication environment in that it allows an individual to repair interactional errors in regard to positive self-concept support and self-concept accuracy. A working knowledge of such a situation can be obtained by examining the following Twenty Question Statement Tests of the real self-concept qualities of a friend-relationship.

First, note once again Bill and John have several real self-concept qualities that allow them to form a friend relationship. Both are intelligent, supportive, hard working, intense, and talkative or persuasive. Second, note that there are several friction points in this relationship. John is critical, manipulative, self-centered, and goal-directed. These qualities along with "forceful" and "persuasive" make anyone a likely target for criticism and manipulation. This is particularly true for someone like Bill who is loyal, caring, and nice. Third, Bill's self-concept qualities

Table 9

Real Self-Concepts for Bill

and John's Friend Relationship

Bill	John
1. Loyal	Forceful
2. Caring	Critical
3. Confrontative	Intelligent
4. Talkative	Manipulative
5. Nice	Intense
6. Intelligent	Persuasive
7. Hard Working	Self-Centered
8. Intense	Goal-Directed
9. Honest	Supportive
10. Supportive	Hard Working

of talkativeness, honesty, and confrontativeness suggest that he will call John's hand. The stability of this relationship will then rest on John's ability to understand the basis of this friendship and his willingness to undertake an interactional repair strategy of accounting when his hand is called. Without such repair strategies this relationship has the potential to be destructive to Bill and to disintegrate. A reassessment of this relationship calls for care in understanding relational re-alignment when criticism, manipulation, and confrontation occur and for the use of relational repairs in order to preserve the relationship.

The Renegotiation of a Relationship

Feelings of friendship are almost always mutual, but sexual attraction may or may not be. In most instances we're not entirely certain how the other person feels, especially since so many people come on strongly for other reasons: to tease, to manipulate, to become sought after. So in order to find out, someone is going to have to show his feelings, and that is when he can get hurt. The one who has to find some way to say, No, I don't feel that way about you, is also uncomfortable because he may not want to jeopardize what has been or could be a good friendship, or simply because he doesn't want to make the other person suffer. He may know that being turned down is a wound that can take a long time to heal. I don't know of an easy way out. Honesty from the beginning seems to help, like pulling adhesive from the skin quickly. The times I have suffered least from being rejected have been with women who didn't stop with no, but who went on to show me how strongly they wanted our friendship to continue, who simply would not allow me to believe I was not liked.

(Prather 1977: 72)

There is perhaps no more stressful experience than being in a potential mate-relationship with another, reassessing the relationship, and coming to the conclu-sion that the relationship needs to be renegotiated to a close friendship. Changes such as this require careful use of one's interactional management skills. Inter-actional management will require the use of accounts, cueing, listening, and negotiating skills and the desire to preserve a close friendship between the indi-viduals involved. Successful interpersonal re-negotiation is dependent upon several interactional management skills. *First*, one must begin by providing strong and accurate positive self-concept support for those qualities of the other's self-concept which will form the basis for the new relationship (Gottman 1979). *Second*, one must isolate carefully those self-concept qualities of the old relationship one wishes to reject. Then one may undertake to re-negotiate the relationship by attempting to explicitly or implicitly reject those qualities. *Explicit* rejection consists of in-dicating that one does not support some specific aspect of the old relationship.

Implicit rejection consists of indicating that one does not support people in general who have the same aspect to their relationship (Dance and Larson 1976). *Third,* one summarizes for the other what effect this rejection has upon the relationship and with an account indicates what the new relationship is that one proposes (Gottman 1979). *Fourth,* one must reaffirm the positive aspects of the other's self which makes the new relationship possible (Gottman 1979). *Finally,* one must suggest that an agreement be made to try this new relationship and express support for the feelings that underly the new relationship (Gottman 1979). Again a working knowledge of such a relational reassessment problem can be gained by examining the following Twenty Question Statement Tests of two individuals' real self-concepts in just such a dating situation.

First, note that both Bill and Jane are honest, intelligent, physically attractive or good looking, good listeners, supportive, strong, theoretic, like jogging, talkative, intense, understanding, like plays, and are enjoyable to be with. It is natural that there will be some mateship attraction based on intelligence and physical attractiveness and some friendship attraction based on intelligence, honesty, strength, theoretic, like jogging, like plays, intense, and enjoyable to be with. It is equally apparent that both provide positive self-concept support and self-concept accuracy for the other. Second, Jane is not in love with Bill and does not find him sexually appealing. Here is a classic case of a dating-relationship which when assessed will disintegrate, but which has the potential to be re-negotiated as a close friend-relationship. What is required is that Jane discuss the issue with Bill by providing

Table 10

Real Self-Concepts for Bill and

Jane's Dating Relationship

Bill	Jane
1. In love with Jane	Not in love with Bill
2. Honest	Honest
3. Intelligent	Intelligent
4. Good looking	Physically attractive
5. Good Listener	Strong
6. Strong	Supportive
7. Supportive	Likes jogging
8. Theoretic	Enjoyable to be with
9. Likes jogging	Good listener
10. Talkative	Intense
11. Intense	Understanding
12. Understanding	Sexy
13. Likes plays	Talkative
14. Enjoyable to be with	Theoretic
15. Helpful	Likes plays

an account for the change in relationship so as to blunt the negative character of the re-negotiation, and then to provide strong and accurate positive self-concept support for establishing the re-negotiated relationship of friend. Since Bill is strong, honest, a good listener, supportive, understanding, and helpful there appears to be a high probability that he can support the change. In addition, their large numbers of common interests and enjoyment of each other's company suggests a motivation for doing so. Here interpersonal relational assessment shows promise of leading to a re-negotiated relationship.

The Disengagement from a Relationship

Last night Rusty pointed out a waitress who was taking orders at the next table. He said that four years ago she was married, had a fourteen-year-old daughter, and was the schools system's consultant on dyslexia. It was summer. She and her husband were having a drink in a bar in Arkansas Pass. Her husband went to the rest room and while he was gone a man at the other end of the bar said, "Hi. Would you like to come with me to Mexico?" On the spot she walked out. She lived with the man for three years in Guatemala. Even more unexpected than the story was the reaction at our table. We were all staring at the woman as if she were a heroine. A time comes when you need to clean house. No, you need to go even further, you need to burn the house down with yourself inside it. Then you must walk away from the fire and say, I have no name.

(Prather 1977: 92)

Since one's self-concept is established and sustained in interaction with others and since the stability and configuration of one's self-concept is the basis for forming interpersonal relationships with others, times may arise when another person has become so destructive to one's self-concept that one's feelings of personal doubt threaten both one's own self and all of one's relationships with others. Such instances invite relational reassessment aimed at disengagement from the destructive interaction pattern (Matthews and Clark 1982). In such instances, four interactional management strategies are available for disengagement: (1) withdrawal/avoidance, (2) concern for positive tone, (3) machiavellianism, and (4) openness (Baxter 1979). In the case of *withdrawal/avoidance* one merely disappears. This strategy is normally used where the feelings of both parties are intense and communication would only serve to fuel comments that would be mutually destructive. *Positive tone* involves undertaking disengagement by providing an account. This allows for the socially appropriate rationalization of the processes. This strategy is employed with individuals who strongly adhere to cultural traditions. *Machiavellianism* involves one individual's manipulating the other into a position where the other must either lose face or break off the relationship. This usually takes the form of a confrontation, fight, or observed deceit regarding some characteristic central to the friend—or mate-relationship. *Finally*, one can be *open* and just tell the other why the relationship is over. This frequently has a devastating effect on the other's self-concept and leads to open conflict or withdrawal. An example of a disengagement problem can be found in the following Twenty Question Statement Test for a husband and wife.

First, note that Don and Kim each are intelligent, physically attractive, and sexually appealing and provide self-concept support for the other. However, note that Don is critical, aggressive, manipulating, cutting, self-centered, mean, and destructive, puts people down, and is confrontative. These qualities are capable of eroding anyone's self-confidence. *Second*, we see that Kim is intelligent, attractive, and sexually appealing, yet insecure, self-derogating, nervous, uptight, and unsure of herself and needs support. In short, her relationship with Don has the potential to destroy the positive aspects of her self-concept by overpowering them with self doubt. Such a situation endangers Kim's self-concept stability and in turn the basis for all her interpersonal relationships. Disengagement from this situation is not only warranted; it is necessary. Relational reassessment indicates the tremendous destructive potential of such relationships.

The four examples of relational reassessment we have considered are in one sense too easy. They involve clear problems which can be resolved by clear strategies. Not all our relational problems will be this simple or clear. In addition, seeing what a problem is and how it can be resolved in no way guarantees that

Table 11

Real Self-Concepts for Don and

Kim—A Husband and Wife Relationship

Don	Kim
1. Critical	Sexy
2. Aggressive	Attractive
3. Intelligent	Insecure
4. Manipulative	Understanding
5. Cutting	Supportive
6. Self-centered	Affectionate
7. Handsome	Needs Support
8. Persuasive	Self-derogating
9. Mean	Nervous
10. Quick	Intelligent
11. Destructive	Helpful
12. Puts people down	Honest
13. Sexy	Uptight
14. Confrontative	Unhappy
15. Supportive	Unsure of self

we will have the emotional detachment or motivation necessary to risk a change in the relationship. Assessing our interpersonal relationships is not always an easy task. Still, such assessments are necessary if we are to exert any measure of control over the growth and disintegration of our self-concepts and interpersonal relationships. Our search for a quality communication environment and a sense of personal worth and relational satisfaction depends in part upon our evaluations and in part on the evaluation of others as to the quality of our relationships. Positive self-concept support, self-concept accuracy, and interactional management skills are essential to that process, as are the awareness and cooperation of others. A failure of any of these elements can do harm to us and our relationships. Awareness of them provides the hope for a satisfactory resolution of our relational problems and a continuation of our relational successes.

Propositions

1. Most Americans report that the quality of their life is determined by the number and quality of their interpersonal relationships.

2. The commonplaceness of friend—and mate-relationships belies the complexity of forming and maintaining these relationships and the loneliness and stress involved when they end.

3. Causes of relational reassessment are numerous, but results of reassessment involve continuation, repair, renegotiation, and disengagement.

4. A quality communication environment provides an opportunity for individual and relational growth, both of which are associated with feelings of self-worth and relational satisfaction.

5. Self-worth and relational satisfaction are the product of perceived self-concept support, self-concept accuracy, and interaction management skills.

6. To provide a presentation of self and/or an attempt to initiate a relationship, an individual presents a confirmation, rejection, or disconfirmation of feedback to another, concerning the other's self or the proposed relationship.

7. A quality communication environment for development of self-worth and relational satisfaction must contain a preponderance of positive self-concept support from others.

8. Self-concept accuracy is essential to predicting the effect of our behavior on others, to achieving an understanding of others, to achieving relational adjustment and to achieving personal and relational happiness.

8. Analysis of Twenty Question Statement Tests of real self-concept characteristics reveals group self-concept support, self-concept accuracy, and interactional management skills.

9. Realignment strategies are socially acceptable vocabularies which affect interpersonal alignment and are essential for interactional management when relationships become problematic.

10. Accounts are particular utterances which attempt to bridge the gap between unanticipated behavior and another's expectations; these accounts realign individual identities and relationships when they are called into question.

11. Successful interpersonal re-negotiation is dependent upon providing strong and accurate positive self-concept support, isolating self-concept qualities one wishes to reject, summarizing the effect the rejection has upon the relationship, indicating what new relationship is proposed, agreeing to try new relationships, and expressing support for feelings underlying the new relationship.

12. Relational assessment aimed at disengagment from the destructive interaction pattern provides for withdrawal/avoidance, positive tone, Machiavellianism, or openness; positive tone provides an account with a socially appropriate rationalization process, and as such may cause the least damage to one's self-concept.

13. Assessment is necessary if we are to exert any measure of control over the growth and disintegration of our self-concepts and interpersonal relationships.

References

Baxter, L. *Relationship Closeness, Relationship Intention and Disengagement Strategies.* Unpublished paper: Speech Communication Association Convention, 1979.

Bernstein, W., and Davis, M. Perspective-Taking, Self Conciousness, and Accuracy in Person Perception. *Basic and Applied Social Psychology.* 3, 1–19, 1982.

Bryant, B., and Trower, P. Social Difficulties in A Student Sample. *British Journal of Educational Psychology.* 44:13–21, 1974.

Campbell, A. *The Sense of Well Being in America: Patterns and Trends.* New York, McGraw Hill, 1980.

Christensen, L., and Wallace, L. Perceptual Accuracy As A Variable In Marital Adjustment. *Journal of Sex and Marital Therapy.* 2:130–36, 1976.

Cissna, K. *Facilitative Communication and Interpersonal Relationships: An Empirical Test of A Theory of Interpersonal Communication.* Unpublished Doctoral Dissertation: University of Denver, CO, 1975.

Clarke, F. *Interpersonal Communication Variables as Predictions of Marital Satisfaction–Attraction.* Unpublished Doctoral Dissertation: University of Denver, CO, 1973.

Corsini, R. Understanding and Similarity in Marriage. *Journal of Abnormal Psychology.* 52, 327–332, 1956.

Dance, F., and Larson, C. *The Functions of Communication: A Theoretical Approach.* New York, NY: Holt, Rinehart and Winston, 1976.

Dryden, W. The Relationships of Depressed Persons. In *Personal Relationships 3*, ed. S. Duck and R. Gilmour, 191–215. New York, Academic Press, 1981.

Duck, S. A Topography of Relational Disengagement and Dissolution. In *Personal Relationships 4*, ed. S. Duck, 1–27. New York, Academic Press, 1981.

Frank, E., and Kupfer, D. In Every Marriage There Are Two Marriages. *Journal of Sex and Marital Therapy*. 2:137–43, 1976.

Gottman, J. *Marital Interaction*. New York, Academic Press, 1979.

Gottman, J., Markman, H., and Notarius, C. "The Topography of Marital Conflict: A Sequential Analysis of Verbal and Nonverbal Behavior". *Journal of Marriage and the Family*. 34:461–477, 1977.

Hill, C., Rubin, A., and Peplau, L. Breakup Before Marriage: The End of 103 Affairs. *Journal of Social Issues*. 32:147–68, 1976.

Larson, C. *Interaction, Dogmatism and Communication Effectiveness*. Unpublished Doctoral Dissertation: University of Kansas, KS, 1965.

Laumann, E. Friends of Urban Men: An Assessment of Accuracy in Reporting the Socio-economic Attributes, Mutual Choice and Attitude Agreement. *Sociometry*. 32:54–69, 1969.

Matthews, C., and Clark III, R. Marital Satisfaction: A Validation Approach. *Basic and Applied Social Psychology*. 3:169–86, 1982.

Montgomery, B. The Form and Function of Quality Communication in Marriage. *Family Relations*. 21–29, 1981.

Murstein, B. *Who Will Marry Whom? Theories and Research in Marital Choice*. Springer, New York: 1976.

Newcomb, M., and Bentler, P. Marital Breakdown. In *Personal Relationships 3*, ed. S. Duck and R. Gilmour, 3, 57–94. New York, NY: Academic Press, 1981.

Orford, J., and O'Reilly, P. Disorders in the Family. In *Personal Relationships 3*, ed. S. Duck and R. Gilmour, 123–40. New York, Academic Press, 1981.

Perlman, D., and Peplau, L. Towards A Social Psychology of Loneliness. In *Personal Relationships 3*, ed. S. Duck and R. Gilmour, 31–52. New York, Academic Press, 1981.

Prather, H. *Notes on Love and Courage*. New York, NY: Doubleday, 1977.

Scott, M., and Lyman, S. Accounts. *American Sociological Review*. 33:46–62, 1968.

Stokes, R., and Hewitt, J. Aligning Actions. *American Sociological Review*. 41:838–49, 1976.

Trower, P. Social Skills Disorder. In *Personal Relationships 3*, ed. S. Duck and R. Gilmour, 97–108. New York, Academic Press, 1981.

Watzlawick, P., Bevin, J., Jackson, D. *Pragmatics of Human Communication: A Study of Interactional Patterns, Pathologies and Paradoxes*. New York, W.W. Norton, 1967.

7

Organizational Communication and Interpersonal Relationships

> The conflict between man and organization has interested so-
> cial philosophers for some time. One of the historical roots of
> this interest can be traced to Rousseau, who saw in institution-
> alization the destruction of man's true and better nature. Karl
> Marx and a number of other sociological theorists have written
> about the frustrations imposed on man by the nature of industrial
> organization. The conflict lies partly in the specialization and
> routinization of mass production and partly in the worker's lack
> of control over his work or over his destiny in the organization.
> According to Marx, the worker is "separated" from the means
> of production, which he does not own, and suffers "alienation"
> . . . a sense of powerlessness and a lack of positive identity with
> his work.
>
> A.S. Tannenbaum (1966:33)

Communication in Organizations

Effective organizational communication enhances overall organizational performance in terms of productivity and member satisfaction. Studies support the common
sense notion that effective communication is one of the top requirements of a
successful mangager (Tubbs and Widgery 1978). Some argue that communication
and management are more or less synonymous (Tompkins 1977). Recognizing the
importance of communication, the Chairman and President of Pitney Bowes holds
annual "job holders' meetings," and the Chairman of United Airlines flies 20,000
miles annually to hold informal discussions with employees, handshaking tours,
and formal meetings. Pitney Bowes is credited with high worker productivity, low
work force turnover, and absence of unionization, and United Airlines is known
for its financial rebound.

We explain organizational communication functionally by referring to the goal
of interaction in which the communication occurs. The function, goal, or purpose
of organizational communication is *production*. That is, the chief concern of organizations is to create and structure communication to enhance output of goods,
services, or information, to coordinate most efficiently tasks related to production,
and to best fit people to these tasks. Therefore, within an organization with its

given resources, communication deals with the coordination of tasks used to produce and market a product or service. The process of sequencing tasks and defining roles within an organization determines the content and structure of communication.

The generative mechanism that maintains and regulates consensus at the organization level is the social unit, which may be the entire organization or a subdivision of it, such as a department or group. Even though the social unit acts as an information network for generating and governing consensus in an organization, its hierarchy as depicted on the organizational chart is structured by the tasks to be performed. While the nature of a specific production task dictates the nature and structure of the social unit, the unit exerts a return impact on task performance. We have all had experience with some social units that were organized in such a manner that they failed to accomplish their tasks. Therefore, with its ability to socialize its members by monitoring consensus and sanctioning agreed-upon actions, the social unit is the generative mechanism for creating and maintaining the coordination of actions in regard to a set of tasks related to production.

How does organizational communication interface with interpersonal communication? Organizational communication establishes a context that influences its members' interpersonal communication and relationships. In addition, organizations and individual workers relate to certain concepts, people, and places in a manner that can result in conflict or cooperation, inefficiency or productivity, and member satisfaction or low morale. In this chapter, we shall look at communication in organizations and the relationship of the individual to the organization in which he or she works; we shall look at the individual's feelings of involvement, loyalty, satisfaction, tension, and conflict, in addition to his or her opposition to, or support of, the formally and informally defined goals and expectations of the organization. Essentially, our interest is in explaining how organizations affect (1) individuals and (2) their interpersonal relationships.

Organizational Communication and the Supervisor-Subordinate Relationship

Federal, state, and local governmental units, universities, colleges, and school systems, corporations and many independent businesses, military units, and medical facilities are complex organizations. Moreover, they differ from one another in the services they provide or goods they produce, in size, in technology, and in the social psychological, administractive-management, and communication assumptions upon which they are based. Regardless, however, of their complexity and differences, Likert and Seashore (1963) found a need for individuals within an organization to view their supervisor-subordinate interaction as supportive and as developing and sustaining the individual's sense of personal worth and importance. Researchers at the University of Michigan's Institute for Social Research interviewed supervisors and subordinates in high- and low-productivity work groups. They found that supervisors in high-productivity groups treated subordinates more as people than as things, animals, or machines for turning out products. Supervisors in low productivity groups were more critical and more punishing, and exercised close rather than general supervision.

The processes involved in initiating and maintaining favorable management-labor interaction, employer-employee communication, or supervisor-subordinate relationships may be viewed as applications of our theoretical perspective on role-taking and self-validation processes presented in Chapters Two and Three. In the case of supervisor-subordinate communication, part of the supervisor's role with respect to subordinates is to reinforce the organization's expectations of the individual. When applied to employer-employee communication, the self-validation process (Cahn 1976 1979; Cahn and Tubbs 1983) describes organizational and supervisor communication situations in which subordinates and supervisors experience a conception of self and the others' experience of that conception. Initially, subordinates and supervisors directly perceive themselves and one another as they experience sensations, interpretations, feelings, intentions, and actions that indicate behavioral, identity, and evaluative real and ideal self-concepts. Through the process of role-taking, in which people imagine the attitudes and expectations others have for them, supervisors and subordinates experience themselves as others view them. Finally, supervisors and subordinates form interpersonal relationships based on each person's comparison of his or her own self-conception with that indicated by the other. This comparison is perceived as self-validating or invalidating.

To better understand the way interpersonal communication functions in organizations, we make three distinctions in regard to supervisor-subordinate communication. They are task, socio-emotional, and innovative in nature. Task communication focuses on how to maintain and enhance productivity given the available resources. Socio-emotional communication focuses on creating and maintaining *esprit de corps*, which results in a high degree of task efficiency and the retention of trained personnel. Innovative communication deals with the changes in production that are needed in order to maintain control over the marketability of the product.

The link between organizational communication and supervisor-subordinate communication becomes clear when we realize that organizations or major subdivisions of organizations may be characterized on the basis of one or more of these communication structures. In some organizations, task communication dominates, as in the case of the military. In others, socio-emotional and innovative communication dominate, as in the civil service and the telecommunication-computer industries, respectively. The implication here is that the social unit determines the consensus that defines and governs the type of communication structure that dominates the organization. For example, a social unit in a task dominated organization issues staff manuals that define roles and announces policies that regulate conduct. There members are taught rigid roles and are punished to the extent that they deviate from them. In organizations that are highly socio-emotionally oriented, the roles are determined by input at regular meetings in which members get together and reinforce their decisions. Furthermore, time, effort, and money are invested in creating favorable member attitudes toward the organization.

We have witnessed sales meetings in which members participated, cheered one another on, and contributed as individuals to the organization's *esprit de corps*. In innovative oriented organizations, the common approach is to select highly competent, creative teams of people who are left free to structure their interrelationships as they please and to do so in such a way as to permit creative ideas to emerge. We hurry to point out that some successful organizations or some subdivisions fit all three of these communication types.

The important point to be made from all this is that we must be able to look at an organization or its subdivision, infer its communication structure, and prescribe the kind of individual who would find such an environment most satisfying. Certainly from an organizaton's point of view, it must determine what type of an organization it is in terms of its communication environment surrounding the task and its sequencing of leadership and work styles in order to screen job and promotion applications for those people who best fit in.

From a member's point of view, one needs to place oneself in an organization or subdivision that best fits one's style. Matching oneself to an appropriate organization includes the ability to analyze oneself and organizations in terms of communication style. One must have this knowledge to understand the kind of place where he or she will flourish and prosper, because different types of self-concepts work at different levels of satisfaction in different communication environments. A perfectionist and workaholic who likes rigid rules and roles may succeed best in a highly task-oriented unit or organization and feel most dissatisfied in a highly socio-emotional unit which appears to waste too much time. If one gets bored quickly, one may want to work in a highly innovative unit or organization where a premium is placed on creativity, a wide range of behavior is tolerated, and the organizational manner is loose and more carefree. Thus, prior to employment, transfer, or a promotion, one must understand oneself as a prime prerequisite to matching oneself with a position in an organization.

We can further illustrate how an employee or a prospective employee might examine his or her self-concept in relation to a specific organization. As in previous chapters, one may find it helpful to complete a Twenty Statement Test and compare it to others. In this case, however, the list of 20 statements should be tailored somewhat to elicit one's preferences on organizational tasks/goals, treatment of a relationship among members, and innovativeness. The following are the real self-concept characteristics of Mike:

helpful	talkative
hard worker	helpful
likes new experiences	thoughtful
likes people	a team player
assertive	friendly
cooperative	intelligent, etc.

Obviously a hard working intelligent person like Mike who is assertive and likes change would pose less of a threat to innovation organizations than to some highly task and socio-emotional oriented organizations. In addition, as a friendly, cooperative team player, Mike might not be well suited for highly competitive jobs in sales where people work for a commission or in the military or in the university where personal recognition is the rule. If you try to analyze yourself in this manner, you will need to also obtain as much information as you can about the organization or specific job that you hold or wish to apply for.

Not only is it desirable to match the individual to an appropriate work organization, but thought must also be given to the management style appropriate to an organization. Traditionally, bureaucratic, administrative, and scientific management theories emphasized supervisor-subordinate relationships based on organizational and cultural self-concepts. Research indicates, however, that effective supervisors relate to subordinates more on appropriative and synesic levels that are interpersonal in nature. Mann and Baumgartel (1952) found that low absenteeism in a power plant was attributed to an open atmosphere in which the foreman took a personal interest in his workers, communicated with them, and "stood up" for them. A theme that undergirds a communication oriented view of management theory prescribes that effective supervisors express warmth and human feeling in ways that are personal and sincere and protect the interests of the employees as well as those of the organization (Gibb 1971; Sieburg 1976).

The self-validation process illustrates a communication-oriented view of management theory and provides a useful and practical understanding of how formal work organizations interact with individual self-conceptions and influence one's interpersonal relationships. Essentially it is a developmental process for relationship growth between supervisors and subordinates. In the following two sections, we will examine the process in the context of two common organizational tasks involving supervisor-subordinate communication, the employment interview, and employee appraisal.

Employment Interview

We begin with the subject of job or employment interviewing because it represents the first opportunity for the development of a subordinate-supervisor relationship. The employment interview is a time in which people (1) consciously explore their behavioral, identity, and evaluative real and ideal self-concepts, (2) intentionally present and sustain in interaction parts of their self-concept, (3) validate perhaps at least some parts of their self-concepts, and (4) form a potential relationship based on the nature and extent of self-validation. Although the interviewer may not be the prospective supervisor, he or she serves to reinforce the organization's expectations in a manner similar to the role served by the supervisor. In addition, at some point in the interviewing process, an applicant eventually meets the prospective supervisor. Therefore, for our purposes, the prospective employer and interviewer are one and the same.

At the first stage of the self-validation process, interviewer A meets applicant B. The purpose of communication at this stage is to present and receive information regarding one another's behavioral, identity, and evaluative real and ideal self-concepts, based primarily on symbolic information received from the past to the present. Each should realize that the scope, depth, and configuration of their self-object relationships constrain the number and type of employers or applicants who can effectively relate to them. For example, if I were a department chairperson at "A" University seeking a teaching position at "B" University, the authoritarian chairperson at B.U., who thinks that I will not knuckle under to his or her forceful control of the faculty, may avoid hiring me. Because supervisor-subordinate relationships depend on the nature of one another's self-concepts, the first stage of the self-validation process is important since it is an opportunity for each to present their self-concepts and perceive the expectations of the other.

At the second stage of the process, each person compares his or her own self-concept with that of the other (the other being one's conception of oneself as viewed by the other), which is based primarily on symbolic information received in this particular situation. Each ascertains an impression that he or she makes on the other, and compares it to his or her own self-concept. If a person finds a significant difference, he or she should determine the reasons for the disparity and work to create a better foundation for future interviews.

At the third stage, interviewer A and applicant B form an interpersonal relationship based on each person's comparison of his or her self-concept and the impression created. At this stage, the interviewer and applicant may experience the mutual realization that they are both being understood. Since a goal of most employment interviews is to develop a favorable interpersonal relationship between the interviewer and applicant, presumably they will attempt to disclose favorable self-concepts which are then received as intended. However, experienced people realize that this is not always the case. They know that the interview can result in an unfavorabe relationship if either of the following two problems occurs: (1) The interviewer or applicant fails to intend to present a favorable self-concept, or (2) the interviewer or applicant intends to display a favorable self-concept, but it is not received by the other as intended.

The self-validation process emphasizes the importance of listening, cueing, and negotiating skills in the employment interview. As described in Chapter Two, these skills improve one's ability to understand others and enable others to make themselves more clearly understood. If their primary purpose is to determine one another's self-object relationships, the interviewer and applicant must *first* be very clear on the type of information they are providing, be it a thought, feeling, intention, or action. It is important that each disclose to the other symbolic information that clarifies his or her relationship to concepts or objects that are important to the other. For example, the interview might reveal how the interviewer and applicant relate to time, work, authority, the employing company, and life style. *Second*, the interviewer and applicant must determine whether one another's statements are asserting or denying (1) their relationships to an object, (2) others' relationship to an object, (3) a characteristic of the object, or (4) a report on someone else's perception of their relationships to an object. *Third*, the interviewer and applicant have available at least two strategies for clarifying their understanding of each other's statements. They can *check out* each other's statements in order to assist self-concept presentation. For example, and applicant dressed in jeans and a T-shirt may be interpreted by some interviewers as indicating disinterest in appearance and sloppy habits. Suppose, however, that when questioned about his or her attire the applicant explains that these clothes conform to the expected dress code of his or her present employment on an assembly line, and there was not enough time to change for the interview. In addition, one may perform *reflective listening* by feeding back to the other what he or she heard or observed. In the above illustration, the interviewer might say to the applicant that he or she now knows that the applicant intends to adapt to the dress code of the prospective employer's working environment. Cueing and listening skills enable both the interviewer and applicant to avoid erroneous assumptions and thereby to enhance accurate perception of the other's self-conception.

Because of the diversity among people, it is common for interviewers and applicants to have divergent and sometimes competing views regarding relationship to objects or self-concept. They need a framework and procedures for dealing with these differences. The negotiation strategies presented in Chapter Two should prove useful. The interviewer and applicant may (1) discover that what were seemingly divergent view points are in fact common perceptions; (2) integrate qualities of both initial positions; (3) use common values to resolve conflicting views; or (4) agree to disagree on the matter at hand.

In summary, the employment interview is important because it sets the stage for the development of favorable supervisor-subordinate relationships. In preparing for and engaging in the employment interview, interviewers and job applicants present and confront their own and one another's behavioral, identity, and evaluative real and ideal self-concepts, a confrontation which results in validating some if not all of the self-concepts presented and forming the basis for relational growth. The process depends on how well each reveals symbolic information that clarifies and specifies the exact nature of his or her relationship to concepts, objects, and people important to the other. Two communication strategies available to both supervisors and subordinates are (1) checking out and (2) reflective listening. Any differences in views need to be negotiated.

Having described the role of interpersonal communication in the employment interview, we next turn to a subsequent task, employee appraisal.

Employee Appraisal

Employee appraisal refers to more or less formal occasions in which supervisors feed back to subordinates an evaluation of their task performance, including attitude, potential, and interpersonal relations. Employee evaluation is an intentional activity serving many purposes: (1) From the supervisor's standpoint, employee evaluation may serve to correct employee deficiencies; (2) it may serve to increase company productivity or image; (3) it may serve to give vent to feelings that harm the supervisor-subordinate relationship; and (4) it may serve to provide information about the employee's definitions and interpretations of important situations. Prior to the evaluation, supervisors may record on an evaluation form an estimate of the employee's performance and attitudes. They may also solicit opinions from other subordinates or supervisors. In any case, they will undoubtedly plan the evaluation to accomplish certain specific goals.

From the employee's standpoint, the evaluation may serve to motivate, guide, reward, and please. At the least, subordinates hope to avoid being discouraged, confused, punished, or offended. Before appearing at the evaluation, subordinates may also talk with other subordinates and supervisors. In addition, they may rehearse some of the statements that they wish to make. Finally, like the supervisor, they may plan the evaluation session to accomplish goals favorable to them.

Because employee evaluation presents a challenge to supervisor-subordinate relationships, it represents a serious area of concern for students of interpersonal communication. If handled improperly, the appraisal may cause the subordinate to feel apathetic toward the job, resulting in lack of cooperation and perhaps in the eventual termination of one's employment. Tactful handling, however, offers opportunities to motivate subordinates, direct their energies toward company goals, and build favorable supervisor-subordinate relationships (Kindall and Getza 1976).

The realization that supervisors can initiate constructive evaluations suggests that the performance of a particular subordinate is the responsibility of the supervisor as well as the subordinate. Meanwhile, different subordinates perceive the supervisor-subordinate relationship differently. Therefore, to form and sustain favorable attitudes and quality performance, the supervisor should direct evaluation efforts at the nature of the supervisor-subordinate relationship as perceived by the individuals involved.

At the first stage of the self-validation process, supervisor A initiates an appraisal of the job performance of subordinate B. Each brings to the appraial interview a self-concept, based primarily on symbolic information received from the past to the present and governing their relationship to objects, people, and places. At the initial stage of the process, the supervisor and subordinate disclose information regarding one another's behavioral, identity, and evaluative real and ideal self-concepts.

At the next stage of the process, the supervisor and subordinate compare their own self-conceptions with the concept each finds the other has formed of him or her: Each needs to know what impression he or she has made on the other, and compares that impression with his or her own self-concept. These comparisons are based primarily on past and present symbolic information.

At the third stage, the nature of the existing supervisor-subordinate relationship may change as a result of each person's comparison of his or her self-concept and the impression created. It is at this stage that the participants may experience the mutual realization that they are both being understood.

As for the employment interview, the self-validation process emphasizes the importance of listening, cueing, and negotiating skills in the formal appraisal. These skills better enable the supervisor and subordinate to understand one another and to make themselves understood. Although supervisors and subordinates can disclose concepts of self by utilizing cueing skills, sometimes they are reluctant to do so. If people fail to disclose themselves to others, they fail to intentionally influence other people's views of them. In such cases their interpersonal relationships are left to chance. If the supervisor's and subordinate's primary purpose is to determine one another's self-object relationships, they must *first* express what they think, feel, want, and do. For example, observation and comments might reveal how each relates to time, work, authority, the employing company, other workers, and life style. Thus, the initial stage of the process fulfills a function by enabling each to disclose to the other symbolic information that clarifies and specifies the nature of the relationship to objects, concepts, or people that are important to one another.

Second, the supervisor and subordinate must determine whether these statements are instances of an identity, behavioral, or evaluative self-object relationship. Only proper cueing by a careful listener can clarify the meaning of such statements. For example, when a supervisor says that something is expected of the subordinate, it may be unclear without further cueing whether this is a report being relayed from above, the supervisor's personal view of the job, or an assertion without any basis at all.

Third, the supervisor and subordinate may use two strategies to clarify each's understanding of statements made by the other. They can *check out* each other's statements to assist self-concept presentation. In addition, they can perform *reflective listening* by feeding back to the other what he or she heard or observed. For example, a subordinate might finish a task and feel good about his or her efforts, but also feel that the supervisor is displeased. Effective questioning should reveal the supervisor's actual position.

Most of us have had the experience of feeling one way about our boss based on day-to-day interaction and feeling less positive toward that person based on his or her criticism of our performance. Criticism of employee behavior presents a particularly difficult problem for the superior who is sincerely concerned about employee self-esteem (Latham and Wexley 1981).

According to the process, supervisors and subordinates should intentionally express their self-concepts to one another. Supervisors should initiate the evaluation session by expressing their self-concepts to the subordinate by speaking for themselves and reporting on what they think, feel, want, and do. Supervisors should also encourage subordinates to express their self-concepts. Supervisors should solicit from subordinates expressions of their self-concepts by asking them to speak for themselves and to report on what they think, feel, want, or do.

To illustrate an application of these interpersonal skills on the job, a fictitious situation will be presented. In the following example, Mrs. Smith is required or wishes to evaluate the performance of her subordinate, John. Suppose that John's performance has not been good. The supervisor is convinced that John's uncooperativeness is the main problem; therefore she invites him to her office. After a few minutes of discussion on John's strengths or other pleasantries, the supervisor changes the topic to focus on John's problem.

Mrs. Smith: Now, John, let me say where I think you can make some improvement. I want to speak frankly and come to the point. Your getting into arguments with others is a problem. I can think of at least two times when I had to step in to settle disputes between you and other employees while on the line. What happened?	Supervisor speaks for herself, making, thinking, feeling, intentional and action-oriented statements.
John: Well, Mrs. Smith, I wanted to do things one way and Joe and Linda had their own ideas. I really wanted the job done well.	Subordinate speaks for himself making intentional and feeling statements.
Mrs. Smith: So do I John. In fact I thought they had some good ideas . . . at least they got the results I wanted. How do you feel about those incidents now?	Supervisor again speaks for herself making intentional and feeling statements.
John: As it turned out, their way worked after all. I guess I made too much of it all.	Subordinate makes feeling statements.

While negotiation involves an accurate understanding of one another's views in order to adjust those views in a way that is mutually acceptable to the participants, sometimes cueing and listening by supervisors and subordinates do not result in the perception of messages as intended. To improve one's accurate understanding of how his or her messages are interpreted by others, supervisors and subordinates need to develop their cueing and listening skills.

Supervisors should solicit from the subordinate validation of the supervisor's self-concept and, where appropriate, validate the subordinate's self-concepts. Recall the previous example with Mrs. Smith and John.

Mrs. Smith: John, it's nice that you want the job done right. This is an area that the company thinks is important too. I also want us all to work together. Constructive suggestions are always welcome, but heated arguments are upsetting to the others, which affects our ability to get the job done. Am I clear on that?

Supervisor states intentions and asks for acknowledgement.

John: Yes. When I say I want to do what's best, I don't really feel that my way has to be the best or only way. I guess when I feel that my ideas don't matter, I lose sight of the fact that the important thing is that all of us work together to get the job done. I'll try to remember that next time.

Subordinate acknowledges supervisor.

Mrs. Smith: Good! I'm glad you see the importance of cooperation as well as doing a good job. What do you hope will happen if you do cooperate more with the others on the line?

Supervisor validates and clarifies.

John: What would I like to see happen? I guess I'd like to see my suggestions get more attention. When I have a good idea, perhaps a change I suggest could even be made.

Subordinate states intention and implies a request for acknowledgment.

Mrs. Smith: I think that can be arranged. I'll talk with Joe and Linda about trying more to implement your ideas, and if they can't for some reason, I'll encourage them to tell you why. You let me know if you feel that your ideas are not getting serious consideration.

Supervisor acknowledges subordinate.

John: That's great! I do like to think that I can have something good to say at least once in a while.

Subordinate confirms and clarifies.

In the preceding example, an interpersonal relationship might have been destroyed if the supervisor and/or the subordinate failed to validate one another's self-concepts. For example, Mrs. Smith might have informed John that she felt that the subordinate was failing to take his job seriously and doing poor work, when John felt otherwise. In response, John might have claimed that the supervisor was not interested in suggestions for improvement and what his employees thought. Furthermore, these criticisms could have been made in the presence of others, adding embarrassment for both. Fortunately, in this example, the supervisor attempted, instead, to employ common sense and the interpersonal communication skills.

The dialogue between Mrs. Smith and John illustrates the kind of expression and validation of self-concepts that leads to the development and maintenance of an interpersonal relationship. The supervisor and subordinate felt and treated each other in a way that was perceived as validating and resolved differences without loss of face. Presumably, John will want to continue working for Mrs. Smith, and both will find the interpersonal aspect of their working relationship mutually validating.

The realization that supervisors can initiate constructive evaluations suggests that the performance of a particular subordinate is the responsibility of both participants. Since each subordinate may perceive the supervisor-subordinate relationship differently, the supervisor should make the effort to create and maintain favorable attitudes along with quality performance by directing evaluation efforts in part toward the relationship as perceived by the individual involved.

In summation, employee appraisal offers opportunities for relational growth and for challenges that require skillful handling. Prior to and during the employee appraisal interview, supervisors who represent the company and their employees present and confront their own and one another's identity, behavioral, and evaluative real and ideal self-concepts, which may or may not result in validation of at least part of their self-concepts. The outcome of the evaluation session depends on how well each reveals symbolic information to the other that clarifies and specifies the nature of self-object relationships important to the other. Both supervisors and subordinates need to use two communication strategies: (1) *checking out* and (2) *reflective listening*. If differences exist in these self-object relationships, they may be negotiated.

Supervisor-Subordinate Communication Problems

Two common supervisor-subordinate communication problems which in turn affect efficiency and productivity are job-related stress and employee alienation. Job-related stress results when two or more supervisors provide a subordinate with inconsistent information. Some communication theorists have discovered that people's opinions and behaviors are influenced by the mean value of the information received from others important to them (Woelfel and Fink 1980). This means that if two or three supervisors give a subordinate conflicting pieces of advice, he or she will probably follow a course of action that represents the mean, average, or compromise of these three points of view, and will suffer some psychological stress. Job-related psychological stress is defined as the emotional arousal experienced when one is confronted with multiple and conflicting expectations from one's superiors.

Linked to psychosomatic illness, cardio-vascular disease, and over consumption of caffeine, tobacco, food, alcohol and drugs, job-related psychological stress is all too common (Rosenman et el. 1975; Caplan 1971; Caplan et al. 1975; Lazarus 1977). In addition, research indicates that people who suffer high levels of role ambiguity and role-conflict tend to communicate less openly and frequently suffer social withdrawal. (Pettigrew et al. 1982; Albrecht 1982).

Since low *esprit de corps* is a sign of high job-related stress, interpersonal communication must be directed at aligning the information from supervisors. There are two ways in which interpersonal communication may reduce job-related stress. First, it may maximize employee interaction through open and supportive lines of communication, informal as well as formal, and through frequent contacts between all levels of an organization, which permit greater opportunities to negotiate differences in expectations among supervisors. Second, it may function as a release valve for conditions that give rise to psychological stress by providing healthy opportunities to constructively discuss frustrations, negative feelings and emotions, and upsetting situations, It should come as no surprise that we recommend communication as the means for reducing psychological stress and enhancing *esprit de corps* in an organization.

Another organizational problem relevant to our discussion is known as "the blue collar blues" . . . job-related alienation which occurs when a worker exerts all his or her energies in one direction and finds that the direction is unimportant. Although an employee does his or her best and expends considerable time and energy, occasionally he or she finds it all wasted. The result is that the person becomes alienated from his or her work and no longer feels proud of it.

When there is a complex task such as making an automobile, television, or applicance, there is a tendency to break down the complex task into simplier subtasks which are easier to perform. Thus, complex tasks are seldom handled by people, but rather are subdivided and reduced to routine tasks. The result is that a person with relatively less education, training, age, and experience can do this simple, standardized task.

When one takes a position on an assembly line to perform a simple routine task, he or she may come to feel that it no longer matters who is performing the task since anyone, regardless of experience, age, and training, can do it. In fact, the person has probably observed or heard that he or she is easily replaceable and that there is a large pool of people waiting in employment lines who are capable of filling his or her role. At least one supervisor has probably told this person that if he or she does not like the job, someone else will gladly take it. When we come to feel that we make little difference in an organization and that anyone can do our jobs, we lose our ideal self in the organization.

Some industries have found ways to cope with the problem of job-related alienation. In some cases, they are able to rotate workers to add variety to their organizational lives. In other cases, they performed an efficiency analysis in which tasks are changed to fit the workers. Jobs need to be as complex as their workers can handle. While tasks can be reduced to extremely simple, routine subtasks, they may also be combined into complex, challenging tasks that workers find more interesting and stimulating. In an efficiency analysis, an organization attempts to adapt and adjust its tasks to the workers.

In instances where industries are unable to make these changes, or if more than these changes are still needed, communication may be the appropriate solution to the problem. First, the communication environment may alter (for the better) workers' self-object relations or perceptions of their jobs. Supervisors can make a subordinate more aware of the importance associated with his or her role in an organization. The fact that one's efforts may save lives, save money, or enhance the industry's image may serve to make the individual feel that the job is important. We are familiar with at least one large corporation that on a regularly scheduled basis informed its employees of the important social and economic contributions the organization was making, a communication that gives its employees something to talk about and to brag about to outsiders. Thus, while jobs did not change in this case, workers' perceptions of them changed due to the industry's communication environment.

Second, the communication environment may alter for the better workers' perceptions of themselves. When supervisors compliment, reward, and recognize a job well done, an individual not only feels more worthwhile but also feels that, as an individual, he or she makes a difference and cannot be replaced by just anyone.

In both solutions involving the organization's communication environment, we focussed on the workers' perceptions . . . either of their jobs or of themselves. Sometimes it is not a person's role or self that is the main contribution to the problem, but rather his or her perceived role or perceived self-concept that is at issue. One may have an important job, but if one does not perceive its importance, the job might just as well be trivial as far as the worker is concerned.

We would like to conclude this chapter by making explicit our position that as long as one knows what others intend, one is in a much better position to adjust to a particular information environment, and that one tends to experience greater difficulty when one does not know what to expect. So, armed with knowledge about one's organizational self-concept and an analysis of an organization's expectations, one can match oneself to the appropriate organization or subunit. If, however, one does not know very much about oneself or one's role expectations, one will probably have problems adjusting to other organizations, if they are different from those with which one is familiar. This may be why the military attempts to "de-individualize" its members to more easily fit them to the available jobs.

Because it is very difficult to match people to jobs, especially when either people or jobs are scarce resources, those adaptive individuals who most easily adjust to the unique demands of different social units may be in a good position to move rapidly up the hierarchy in a particular field or organization. Usually, broad education and varied experiences contribute to one's ability to adapt and grow.

The role relationships that you desire and those dictated by the organization require that you understand yourself and the organization's communication structure or style, that you listen to what the organization expects from its members or employees, and if the match between the individual and the organization is less than desired, that you cue your superiors and negotiate the difference. One may negotiate how one performs a task, what hours one works, how one relates to supervisors, subordinates, and co-workers, and so on. Thus, interpersonal communication skills become increasingly important in a tight job market, especially for those who find that they have too many years invested in their place of work to make a move somewhere else.

Propositions

1. Effective communication enhances overall organizational performance in terms of productivity and member satisfaction.

2. The function, goal, or purpose of organizational communication is production.

3. The generative mechanism which maintains and regulates consensus at the organizational level is the social unit, which may be the entire organization or a subdivision of it, such as a department or group.

4. Organizational communication establishes a context that influences its members' interpersonal communication and relationships.

5. The processes involved in initiating and maintaining favorable supervisor-subordinate relationships may be viewed as applications of our theoretical perspective on role-taking and self-validation processes presented in Chapters Two and Three.

6. Supervisor-subordinate communication may be task-oriented, socioemotional, and/or innovative in nature.

7. One may look at an organization, identify the type of supervisor-subordinate communication that dominates, and prescribe the kind of individual who would find such a communication environment most satisfying.

8. In addition to properly matching individuals to organizations, thought must also be given to the management style appropriate to an organization.

9. The self-validation process illustrates a communication-oriented view of management theory and provides a useful and practical understanding of how formal work organizations interact with individual self-concepts and influence one's interpersonal relationships.

10. The employment interview is examined as a self-validation process because it represents the first opportunity for the development of a supervisor-subordinate relationship.

11. The appraisal of employees is also examined as a self-validation process because it presents a serious challenge to supervisor-subordinate relationships.

12. As self-validation processes, the employment interview and employee appraisal emphasize the importance of listening, cueing, and negotiating skills.

13. Communication is recommended as the means for reducing job-related psychological stress and enhancing *esprit de corps* in an organization.

14. Communication is also recommended for reducing job-related alienation.

15. It is our position that as long as one knows what others expect, one is in a much better position to adjust to a particular information environment, and that one tends to experience greater difficulty when one does not know what to expect.

Note

1. Portions of this chapter were taken from Cahn, D.D., "The Employment Interview: A Self-Validation model,"*Journal of Employment Counseling*, December, 1976, pp. 150–55: Cahn, D.D., "Employee Evaluation as a Self-Validation Process," *Journal of Employment Counseling*, March, 1979, pp. 31–37; Cahn, D.D. and Tubbs, S., "Management as Communication: Performance Evaluation and Employee Self-Worth," *Communication*, 1983, 12 (3), 46-54.

References

Albrecht, T.L. Coping with Occupational Stress: Relational and Individual Strategies of Nurses in Acute Health Care Settings. In *Communication Yearbook 6*, M. Burgoon. Beverly Hills, CA: International Communication Association, 1982.

Cahn, D.D. The Employment Interview: A Self-Validation Model. *Journal of Employment Counseling*. 13:150–55, 1976.

Cahn, D.D. Employee Evaluation as a Self-Validation Process. *Journal of Employment Counseling*. 16:31–7, 1979.

Cahn, D.D., and S. Tubbs., Management as Communication: Performance evaluation and Employee Self-Worth, *Communication*. 12 (3):46–54, 1983.

Caplin, R. Organizational Stress and Individual Strain. Unpublished Doctoral Dissertation. Ann Arbor, MI: University of Michigan, 1971.

Caplin, R., Cobb, S., French, J.R.P., Harrison, R.V., and Pinneau, S.R. *Job demands and Worker Health*. Washington, D.C.: HEW Publication No. (NIOSH) 75–160, 1975.

Gibb, J.R. Defensive Communication. *Journal of Communication*. 11:141–48, 1971.

Kindall, A.F., and Gatza, J. Positive Program for Performance Appraisal. In *Communication in Organizations*, ed. J. Owen, P. Page, and G. Zimmerman. New York, NY: West, 1976.

Latham, G.P., and Wexley, K.N. *Increasing Productivity through Performance Appraisal.* Reading, MA: Addison-Wesley, 1981.

Lazarus, R.S. Psychological Stress and Coping in Adaptation and Illness. In *Psychosomatic medicine*, ed. Z.J. Lipowski, D.R. Lipsitt, and P.C. Whybrow. New York, NY: Oxford University Press, 1977.

Likert, G. and Seashore, C. Making Cost Control Work. *Howard Business Review.* 41(6), 96–108, 1963.

Mann, F. and Baumgartel, H.G. *Absences and Employee Attitudes in an Electric Company.* Ann Arbor: Survey Research Center, U. of Mich., 1952.

Pettigrew, L.S., Thomas, R.C., Ford, J., and Costello, D.E. The Effects of Job Related Stress on Medical Center Employee Communicator Style. In *Communication Yearbook 5*, ed. M. Burgoon, N. Brunswick, NJ: International Communication Association, 1982.

Rosenman, R.H., Brand, R.J., Jenkins, C.D., Friedman, M., Straus, R., and Wurm, M. Coronary Heart Disease in the Western Collaborative Group Study: Final Follow-Up Experience of 8½ Years. *J.A.M.A.* 233:872–77, 1975.

Sieburg, E. Confirming and Disconfirming Organizational Communication. In *Communication in Organizations*, ed. James L. Owen, Paul A. Page, and Gordon I. Zimmerman. St. Paul, MN: West, 1976.

Tannenbaum, A.S. *Social Psychology of the Work Organization.* Belmont, CA: Wadsworth, 1966.

Tompkins, P.K. Management Qua Communication in Rocket Research and Development. *Communication Monographs.* 44:1–26, 1977.

Tubbs, S.L., and Widgery, R.N. When Productivity Lags, Check at the Top: Are Key Managers Really Communicating? *Management Review.* 67:20–25, Dec. 1967.

Woelfel, J., and Fink, E.L. *The Measurement of Communication Processes: Galileo Theory and Method.* New York, NY: Academic Press, 1980.

8

Cultural Communication and Interpersonal Relationships

> No one has been able to define exactly how a culture integrates
> and homologizes the ideas and actions of many men over long
> periods of time anymore than how the consciousness gives a
> thematic continuity to the life of an individual. As far as one
> can tell, the collective consciousness of the group creates a mode
> of looking at the world or arrives at some imaginative visual
> bearing. At the center there lies a "tyrannizing image" which
> draws everything toward itself. This image is the ideal of its
> excellence.
>
> Richard Weaver (1964:11–12).

Culture: A Tyrannizing Image

A culture is a complex of values polarized by an image containing a vision of its own excellence. Such a "tyrannizing image" takes diverse forms in various cultures such as "rugged individualism" in America, an individual's "harmony with nature in Japan" and "collective obedience" in China. A culture's tyrannizing image provides its members with a guide to appropriate behavior and posits a super-sensible world of meaning and values from which even its most humble members can borrow to give a sense of dignity and coherence to their lives. From within this vision, from this ideal of its own excellence, comes the culture's power to cohere, to inspire, and to motivate collective action consistent with its ideals. The term "tyrannizing image," devoid of its sinister connotations, captures this notion of a centripetal, unifying, and compelling power. Every culture relies upon this power to deal with the inevitable tensions which arise between the impulse of individuals to be free and the need of society for an orderly communal life. Similarly, each member of society has a desire to be at once an individual set apart from others by a sense of personal worth, and at the same time a member of a community with a sense of communal worth. A tyrannizing image, to function effectively, must be capable of uniting society's members under common values while making provisions for individual differences. A proper balance between these interests provides the members of a culture with satisfaction in the knowledge that society has roles for various kinds of people and that the performance of those roles creates a kind of symphony of labor, play, and social life while allowing pride in and respect for individual differences (Weaver 1964).

119

While the content and form of a given culture's tyrannizing image is a product of its past history, current consensus, and future vision, the power or capacity of that image to gain adherence and to regulate action is created and sustained in and through cultural communication processes. It will be the purpose of this chapter to explore: (1) the role of culture in communication, (2) the role of interpersonal communication in American culture, (3) the role of American culture in marital relationships, and (4) the cultural repair ritual for marital problems.

Culture and Communication

Philipsen (1981) notes that a culture's ability to integrate and homologize the ideas and actions of individuals is dependent upon its capacity to employ communication to resolve three specific problems. First, cultural communication must provide for the coordination of diverse individuals into common lines of action in order to perform necessary community functions. This is the problem of *alignment*. Second, cultural communication must provide a consistent and compelling vision of its cultural ideals, or tyrannizing image, in order to motivate and reward significant communal action. This is the problem of *meaning*. Third, cultural communication must provide standards for appropriate role performance and the distribution of communication between roles in order to provide for a sense of cultural place and organizational hierarchy. This is the problem of *form*.

Problems of alignment, meaning, and form are dealt with according to Philipsen (1981) through such communication forms as ritual, myth, and social drama. A *ritual*, according to Turner (1980), is a patterned sequence of symbolic action, the correct performance of which constitutes homage to the culture's sacred object. Marriage ceremonies, Independence Day celebrations, and national elections are instances of American cultural rituals paying homage to marriage, the Declaration of Independence, and democratic institutions. According to Philipsen,

> Rituals function so as to maintain the consensus for social equilibrium and order, especially the nonrational consensus. Their form provides for the celebration of what is shared by participating in known sequences of coordinated actions, which by definition, require . . . and, once enacted, implicate . . . the exploitation of shared rules. Thus, ritual, the most highly precoded of the cultural communication forms, is a declaration of form against indeterminacy.

> (Philipsen 1981:7)

A *myth*, according to Levi-Strauss (1970), is a symbolic narrative which captures a culture's core values and has a grip on the communal imagination. Myths provide a model of appropriate cultural action to which members of a culture can orient themselves to give purpose and dignity to their lives. King Arthur's Camelot, George Washington's chopping down a cherry tree, and President Lincoln's freeing the slaves are examples of cultural myths which hold a grip on the American imagination. According to Philipsen,

> Myths posit a supersensible world of meaning and values from which the least member of a tribe can borrow something to dignify and give coherence to his life. Whereas ritual is the form whereby cultural actors most directly and most wholeheartedly affirm the past, the traditional, myth is the form wherein they creatively apply and discover the fit between past and present, community and individual. They can use myth to give life coherence, by seeing their own acts as conforming to a pattern which is implicit in the patterned stories of the heroic figures of their tribes past.

(Philipsen 1981:8)

A *social drama*, according to Turner (1980), is a dramatic presentation of a breach in cultural values, the crises it causes, the redress of the offender, and the reintegration of the offender into the community or the community recognition of a moral dissensus. The cultural disruptions of the Civil War, Watergate, and the deaths of Martin Luther King and John F. Kennedy are examples of American social dramas in which cultural values were called into question and then reaffirmed, or in which a recognition of a moral dissensus emerged. According to Philipsen,

> Social dramas play an important function in communal life. Whereas rituals have as their dominant function the celebration of a code, and myths have as theirs the using of the code to make sense of the communal conversations, social dramas serve as occasions for defining the boundaries of the group and for reintegrating into the group those individuals whose acts have tested the community's moral boundaries. Whereas ritual is a way to affirm it, and myth is a way to articulate and apply it, a social drama is a way to remake and negotiate a particular people's sense of communal life.

(Philipsen 1981:9)

In Chapter One, we defined cultural communication in terms of the function it serves, namely the regulation of consensus with respect to institutions . . . i.e. established values, beliefs, assumptions, and behavioral expectations. These institutions underlie the sense of unity that members of a culture share. An understanding of ritual, myth, and social drama and how they function can lead to an understanding of cultural institutions and the influence cultural communication exerts upon interpersonal communication processes. We will next attempt to locate the central communication rituals, myths, and social dramas that influence interpersonal relationships. In so doing we shall explore how our culture balances the interests of the individual and the culture in dealing with such problems in interpersonal communication as alignment, meaning, and form, in order to provide its members with a sense of personal and cultural worth.

Interpersonal Communication in American Culture

There is some concern in western society as a whole and in American society in particular that the interplay between the individual and communal interests has in the past ten years experienced a sharp increase in favor of individual power and a concomitant decline in communal power. This rise in individualism, it is argued, has shifted the locus of control for solving problems of communal alignment, meaning, and form away from a culture's tyrannizing image towards the individual's ideal self-concept. Three broad shifts have been cited as evidence of our culture's declining power over its members and their interpersonal relationships.

Sennett (1976) and Berger et al. (1974) pinpoint one such change when they claim that the center of moral gravity has shifted from the public to the intimate domain, thereby changing the locus of control in solving problems of *alignment*. They argue forcefully that public standards of correct behavior have given way to individual standards. This has led, in turn, to a shift away from the appeal to common cultural values in solving alingment problems to a relative emphasis on negotiation between and among intimates to correct such problems. Berger et al. (1974) note that one significant implication of such a change is that "honor" has been replaced by "dignity" as an ultimate term in our social vocabulary. The ascribed status of the community or honor has given way to the personal status of the individual. It is argued that:

> The social location of honor lies in a world of relatively intact, stable institutions, a world in which individuals can with subjective certainty attach their identities to the institutional roles that society assigns to them. The disintegration of this world as a result of the forces of modernity has not only made honor an increasingly meaningless notion, but has served as the occasion for a redefinition of identity and its intrinsic dignity apart from and often *against* the institutional roles through which the individual expresses himself in society. The reciprocity between individual and society, between subjective identity and objective identification through roles, now comes to be experienced as a sort of struggle. Institutions cease to be the "home" of the self; instead they become oppressive realities that distort and estrange the self. Roles no longer actualize the self, but serve as a "veil of *maya*" hiding the self not only form others but from the individual's own consciousness.

> (Berger et al. 1974:93–94).

Berger et al. (1974) have suggested, secondly, that this shift in the locus of power from the cultural to the personal domain has led to a loss of cultural meaning which is expressed in a widespread sense of "homelessness":

The individual is given enormous latitude in fabricating his own particular private life . . . a kind of "do-it-yourself" universe.—This latitude obviously has its satisfactions, but it also imposes severe burdens. The most obvious is that most individuals *do not know how* to construct a universe and therefore become furiously frustrated when they are faced with a need to do so. The most fundamental function of institutions is probably to protect the individual from having to make too many choices. The private sphere has arisen as an intersitial area left over by the large institutions of modern society. As such, it has become underinstitutionalized and therefore become an area of unparalleled liberty and anxiety for the individual. Whatever compensations the private sphere provides are usually experienced as fragile, possibly artificial, and essentially unreliable.

(Berger et al. 1974:186–7).

Finally, when the locus of control shifts from the cultural or public to the individual or private domain, standards for role fulfillment and the distribution of appropriate communication in the culture decline, substituting individual *form* for cultural form. It is argued that:

Today, the stress is on "saying all," on telling "how it is," in explicit rebuttal to what are regarded as archaic, class-determined, uptight atavisms of censorship and decorum.—The approved loquacities of psychoanalysis, of mundane confession (as they are practiced in modern therapy), in modern literature, in competitive gregariousness, and on the media go directly counter to the ideals of communicative reticence or autonomy represented by the private letter, diary, or journal. The telephone consumes, with utter prodigality, raw materials of language of which a major portion was allocated to internal use or to the modulated inwardness of the private, silently conceived written correspondence. One is tempted to conclude that where much more is, in fact, being heard, less is being said.

(Steiner 1967:208)

The shift in locus of control from cultural to individual in solving problems of alignment, meaning, and form leads to a general challenging of culture myths, rituals, and social dramas by major segments of American culture. The significance of such a challenge by the individual to a culture's norms is nowhere more apparent than in the regulation of marital relationships in America.

American Culture and Marital Relationships

Whereas a culture's tyrannizing image seeks in some sense to influence the character of almost all types of interpersonal relationships among its members by specifying the ideal characteristics of friends and mates, one type of interpersonal relationship which a culture finds significant enough to regulate by law is the marital relationship. The regulation of marital relationships is of the utmost importance to a culture in terms of its distribution of resources, family organization, and sense of hierarchy. In short, the paradigm case of cultural influence in the interpersonal arena is in its attempt to regulate marital relationships. It is by examining the cultural myths, rituals, and social dramas designed to regulate this process that we will obtain our clearest vision of cultural communication at work in balancing individual and collective interests in influencing interpersonal relationship processes.

Our culture legally recognizes two distinctly different marital patterns . . . a traditional type based on collective interests and a contemporary alternative type based on individual interests. Each type is marked by its own set of myths, rituals, and social dramas (Blood and Blood 1979). Observers point to the rise in individualism and in women's liberation as the central influences on the emergence of the contemporary alternative to the traditional pattern. Before exploring each pattern in some detail, it is important to begin by examining their common roots.

Recall that in Chapter Four we examined the mate selection process. In that discussion we outlined the ritual most Americans employ in selecting a mate. First, they select persons of the opposite sex whom they perceive as intelligent, physically attractive, sexually appealing, and possessing a common set of cultural characteristics. It is also noteworthy that these are matching qualities, which means that individuals select others who are about the same as they believe they are in regard to those qualities, thus allowing for individual differences in applying the cultural standards. Second, individuals select another as a mate in the belief that the other conforms to their ideal image of a mate. What that image is may vary, but that a relevant other must conform to it is a culturally prescribed influence. Third, both parties involved must perceive the male's real and ideal self-concept as being close to one another. Fourth, such a proposal of relationship to the other must have a likelihood of success. Finally, progress in the mate selection process from casual date to mate must be dependent upon reciprocal self-concept support and self-concept accuracy.

In America most first marriages take place when the male is 24 and the female 22 years old. Ninety-two percent of all women marry by age 30, and 97% of all women marry at least once. So, there appears to be a strong and persistent influence in our culture for individuals to enter into marital relationships (Hacker 1979). However, while most Americans follow the same mate selection pattern and feel considerable pressure to do so at an early age, the myths governing marriage, the rituals that involve initiation and maintenance, and the social dramas that are involved in their termination follow two quite different paths, one being traditional and the other the contemporary alternative. Let us examine each in turn.

Traditional marital patterns. Traditional marital relationships are symbolized in the wedding vow to marry for better or worse, until death do us part. Ideal mates are defined by their adherence to the traditional roles of the society as husband and wife, father and mother, family provider and obedient spouse. Such marriages begin by obtaining a license, then by participating in a marriage ceremony which is considered a legal contract and by taking the traditional marriage vows of (1) giving up private property in favor of communal property, (2) renouncing all sexual partners save the spouse, and (3) the male acting as economic provider and the female as obedient servant (Blood and Blood 1979). This, then, is the myth underlying traditional marital relationships. Idealized cultural duties and obligations guide perceptions of marital relationships.

Traditional marital relationships reflect a style involving a four-stage ritual. The first stage is termed *magical* in that each partner acts and is motivated by the idealized cultural images involved in the agreement to marry, the wedding, and the honeymoon. The second stage is termed *idealized conventional* as each partner attempts to learn and perform the various aspects of the cultural role of husband and wife, provider and servant, and male and female sex partner. The third stage is termed *individualistic* as each partner begins to pursue his or her own interests, values, and emotions. The fourth stage is termed *affirmational* as each begins to understand and find significance in the other's unique self without relying on social conventions to guide interactions (Tamashiro 1978).

Researchers point out that about 60% of American marriages follow a traditional pattern, 58% last more than 15 years, 52% more than 20 years, 47% more than 25 years and 16% more than 50 years (*Newsweek* 1981). Most of these marriages show a general decline in expression of affection and problems over time (Swensen, Eskew, and Kohlhepp 1981). They become very routine and are frequently termed "American Gold Watch Marriages—short on excitement and fulfillment, but long on security (*Newsweek* 1981).

While the dissolution of such marriages is infrequent, the social drama involved is quite clear. Traditionally, such marriage contracts are broken by a partner's (1) committing the crime of adultery, (2) squandering communal property on drink or riotous living, or (3) being disobedient with rebellious behavior. Any such violation of the marriage vows provides a legal basis for divorce or fault on the grounds of breach of contract. The offended partner and children are seen as innocent victims of presumed criminal acts. The offended party is bitter and angry and the offender is condemned by the courts, leaving a feeling of guilt. The social drama involved in the divorce is bitter and painful. Typically, the parent and children involved cut off their relationship with the violator and deal with offender indirectly through an attorney, with the public and the court seeing that the violator pays for his or her evil deeds in child support, property, and custody of the children (Blood and Blood 1981).

Alternative marital patterns. Non-traditional marital patterns are symbolized in wedding vows that are conditional in nature, frequently built on a consensus formed during a stage of cohabitation prior to marriage as a test of a relationship. That test is designed to see if living together proves mutually beneficial to individual growth and development. If living together proves mutually beneficial, then they may decide to legalize the relationship by marriage. Once formalized, the relationship should last only "so long as we both shall love." Marriage is dissolved immediately if life begins to become worse than it would be apart. Both sexes view the relationship as among equals with common property, implied sexual exclusivity to the spouse and role dominance being of little concern. Rather, the chief commitment is to the other as a respected individual. But this commitment remains conditional on their own development and commonality of direction. This, then, is the myth that underlies the alternative marital relationships . . . idealized individual development and personal relationship satisfaction (Blood and Blood 1979).

Non-traditonal marital relationships reflect a different style involving a different four stage ritual. First, the spouses are typically *self-centered* and think of the relationship only in terms of their own individual interests. Second, they begin to recognize differences in each other's individual interests and negotiate *quid pro quo*–a service for a service, a concession for a concession. Third, they begin to appreciate each other's individuality and make accomodations for the good of the relationship. Fourth, they evolve a set of "rules of the relationship" by which to avoid problems (*Newsweek* 1981).

Researchers tell us that, unfortunately, this type of relationship seldom gets beyond stage two. Divorce and separation is common in this pattern, as are extramarital affairs and remarriage (*Newsweek* 1981). Frequently, the marriage is childless and occupationally rather than family oriented (Vaughan 1979). Such marriages are frequently exciting and intense, but only for short periods of time.

While the breakup of such relationships is common, the consequences to the partners involved are not punishing and may even be rewarding. Divorce in this context is normally no-fault. It reflects respect for individual growth and a realization that couples may grow apart. The normal circumstances for ending such relationships without fault are three. First, partners who are initially compatible become incompatible because one partner changes in a way that the other finds intolerable. Second, partners change not their values but the ranking of those values. Third, partners have a conflict from the beginning which becomes more severe. In each case staying together is a strain on the individual, requiring one partner to sacrifice a significant aspect of self. Divorce solves the problem by allowing for personal growth. Frequently, such strains lead to amicable divorce where those involved de-escalate the relationship from mate to close friend, date, or lover. Where each retains individual property and where communal property is split or shared, children are allowed equal access to both parents, who may accept a shared responsibility for their children's development and finances. In such cases, exmarrieds frequently maintain common friendship and relative relationship patterns. Marriages end, and people no longer assume that their relationships with each other must end (Blood and Blood 1979). Less than 20% of American marriages are of this type, while the remaining 20% tend to be a mixture, beginning as a contemporary alternative type and ending in the traditional pattern. However, those involved in the alternative type tend to be more educated, liberal, and non-religious and have a relative higher income than those involved in traditional marriages (Hacker 1979).

The traditional and contemporary alternative types of marriage are illustrated by couples 1 and 2, respectively, as depicted in Table 12.

For each couple, the husband and wife have listed real self-concept statements relevant to their marriages. Bill and Sue, couple #1, exemplify couples who are wedded in a traditional manner. Their primary role characteristics are traditional. They easily see themselves as married, in the social roles of husband and wife, with all the qualities that go with these traditional roles. Sue admires her husband, wants to have children, wants to be a homemaker, wants to help her husband. Bill, on the other hand, sees himself as a provider, a family man, with traditional aspirations. While couple #1 manifests cultural aspects of real self-concepts that are embedded in the traditional marriage type of interpersonal relationship, the real self-concepts of couple #2, Rita and Frank, are indicative of couples who are wedded according to the contemporary alternative type of marriage. Their primary roles are lawyer and teacher, not husband and wife. They are in love and happy, but more concerned about themselves as individuals rather than as cultural roles. Problems would emerge if persons with these different views of marriage were to meet and seek to establish a mate-relationship.

What then can we conclude from our inquiry into the cultural regulation of marital relationships? First, it seems clear that the traditional marriage is still a dominant pattern and is very much regulated by American's cultural image of marital excellence. However, that control is declining, with 38 out of every 100 marriages ending in divorce, 29 of these marrying again, and 13 of those 29 getting divorced again. In addition there have been dramatic increases in the number of people choosing not to marry but rather choosing to cohabit (Hacker 1979). Second, it seems clear that the alternate pattern of marital relationships is growing rapidly among the most affluent and well educated Americans, offering a powerful challenge to the traditional cultural pattern. In addition, the legal recognition of a no-fault divorce provides recognition for the legitimacy of this challenge (Blood and Blood 1979). Third, as we shall see in the next section, our culture has become very concerned about the relationship problems which arise from the conflict between the need of culture for orderly collective action and the need of the person for individual development. Thus, a culturally sanctioned myth, ritual, and social drama has emerged which has as one of its principle functions the resolution of such conflicts in interpersonal relationships.

Weaver (1964) argues that one can characterize a culture's inability to live up to its tyrannizing image or cultural ideal by the dominant types of repair rituals which occur among its members. Such rituals allow the individual members of a culture who fail to approximate the cultural ideals to rationalize that failure in a way that affirms the necessity of the ideal while preserving the integrity of the individuals involved. Thus, in Asia there are repair rituals for saving public face, in Europe there are repair rituals for failing to be worldly, and in the United States there are repair rituals for not living up to the cultural ideals on marriage.

Table 12

Twenty Question Statement Test on Two Married Couples

COUPLE ONE		COUPLE TWO	
Sue's Real Self	Bill's Real Self	Rita's Real Self	Frank's Real Self
1. I am married	1. I am married	1. I am a lawyer	1. I am a teacher
2. I am a wife	2. I am a husband	2. I am in love	2. I am in love
3. I am in love	3. I am a provider	3. I want to be attorney general	3. I am intelligent
4. I have a nice husband	4. I am in love	4. I want a house	4. I am happy
5. I am attractive	5. I am intelligent	5. I want to travel	5. I want to travel
6. I want to have children	6. I want to have a family	6. I want my own law firm	6. I want a house
7. I want a house	7. I want to own a house	7. I am an individual	7. I want to write books
8. I want to help my husband be successful	8. I want my kids to go to college	8. I am sexy	8. I am handsome
9. I am happily married	9. I am happy	9. I am happy	9. I am a strong person
10. I am intelligent	10. I am thoughtful	10. I am intelligent	10. I am hard working

The Cultural Repair Ritual for Marital Problems

Regardless of whether couples attempt to live up to the ideals of the traditional marital pattern or of the contemporary alternative type, they are bound to experience interpersonal problems. How are these problems dealt with in the American culture? Katriel and Philipsen (1981) outline the elements involved in an interpersonal communication ritual that functions as a repair sequence for dealing with break-downs in marital communication regardless of type, traditional or contemporary. To understand more fully how this ritual is a cultural manifestation of deep-seated American beliefs, assumptions, and values, we must first examine how Americans view interpersonal communication, and how they view its role in relationship development or in interpersonal bonding. While communication theorists and re-searchers may have their own ideas on these subjects, we must learn how our culture views them in order to discover the interpersonal communication ritual used to resolve interpersonal problems in American culture.

Employing an ethnographic analysis of several cultural texts, Katriel and Phi-lipsen (1981) found that the term "communication" in the interpersonal context refers to close, supportive, and flexible speech. Interpersonal communication func-tioned as work necessary to self-definition and interpersonal bonding. Finally, they delineated the elements involved in an interpersonal communication ritual. Let us briefly explore each of these findings.

First, communication in its interpersonal context is separated from "mere talk," "normal chitchat," or "small talk" by its *close* rather than distant character. In-terpersonal communication is a medium of interchange between close friends or intimates. It involves the interpenetration of the unique self-conepts of those involved. To allow for such an interpenetration, each person involved must disclose information about his or her unique self-image. Mere talk, chit-chat, and small talk is distant in that it is about people and objects external to the interaction and is not dependent upon the unique self-image of those interacting.

Second, interpersonal communication is separated from mere talk by its *sup-portive* rather than neutral tone. To engage in interpersonal communication one need not approve everything another presents, but one must support the other as a unique self or an important individual. Positive regard is essential for such interactions. In mere talk we find an absence of such committment to and regard for the other. Such an absence may either take the form of neutrality or negative self-regard.

Third, communication in its interpersonal context is flexible rather than rigid interaction. Here flexibility refers to a willingness to listen, acknowledge, and understand the others presentation of self and to consider changing one's perception of self dependent upon the meaning which emerges from the interaction. In short, self and relationship emerge from the interaction and are contingent upon the close, supportive, and flexible characteristics of those involved. Mere talk is governed by social conventions and social roles apart from the ideal self-concepts of the interactants.

How does interpersonal communication function as the work necessary for self-definition and interpersonal bonding? Here the term "work" requires further explication. In our culture the terms "self," "relationship," and "communication" designate categories of events which can be analyzed, taken apart, evaluated, and then put back together in an improved form. This process of analysis, disassembly, and reassembly through speech is termed "work." Americans work on their communication, self-concept, and relationships in order to improve them. However, such work requires communicative competence or knowledge of self-concept and communication skill. One's work ethic and competence is judged by the quality of one's communication environment, self-concept, or interpersonal relationships. When one's work ethic and communication competence are low, we experience communication, self-concept, and relational break-downs or situations requiring repair. When one's work ethic and communication competency is high, we experience communication, self-concept, and relational growth.

Finally, Katriel and Philipsen (1981) outline the elements involved in the interpersonal communication repair ritual. They claim that the specific set of expectations and sequences involved in "sit down and talk," "work out a problem," or "discuss our relationship" function as a culturally preferred way of paying homage to a sacred object . . . the definition of self experienced by any one of the interactants, usually the one who initiates the sequence. The *topic* of such an interaction is one's experience of one's self and one's world. The simultaneous awareness of an individual's uniqueness and one's world view requires confirmation by others. This need for validation is the *purpose* of interpersonal communication which seeks its validation in the response of close, supportive, and flexible others. These friends or intimates constitute the *participants* in the ritual. The *setting* is one where talk is the primary activity, privacy prevails, and the participants can be involved with one another. The *norm of interaction* consists of feeling that communication is important and that the couple should "sit down and talk."

The ritual itself appears to unfold in the following four steps. First, there is an initiation step in which one member announces the existence of a personal problem which can only be worked out in communication. Ruth, who has been left home alone for several evenings by her husband, Tim, feels that she can no longer passively sit home and must confront her husband today. She initiates the ritual by selecting the appropriate time and place where they can sit down and talk, and brings up the problem. Second, there is an acknowledgement step where the relevant other indicates a willingness to discuss this personal problem, thereby acknowledging its legitimacy. Tim responds to Ruth by indicating his willingness to engage in the repair activity. Thus, Tim indicates his cooperativeness by sitting down and talking. Third, there is a negotiation step where the problem is stated and explored from multiple points of view. As the initiator of the ritual, Ruth would do a lot of self-disclosing, and Tim would indicate his cooperation by listening with non-judgmental, non-inquisitive empathy. Ruth's attitude is one of acceptance to both feedback and suggestions for change. Finally, there is a reaffirmation step in which the uniqueness of the individual is affirmed and the solution located is found to be consistent with some valued principle of the initiator's self-concept, thus mitigating any threat to the initiator's identity. The fact that compromises are not always possible is seen as threatening to the relationship. Ruth and Tim must clarify for each other and examine together the discrepant positions, personal needs, and individual interpretations, but they must reaffirm their relationship to lessen the interpersonal threat posed by these differences.

Interpersonal communication functions as work necessary to self-definition and interpersonal bonding (relationship development) and is depicted in the American culture as a ritual for repairing relationship and marital problems. The significance of this ritual for Americans in dealing with relationship problems in general and marital relationships in particular is attested to by its frequent occurrence in everyday activity, its frequent use in sitcoms, soap operas, and talk shows on TV, and its use in endless counseling programs aimed at self and relationship enhancement.

Propositions

1. A culture is a complex of values polarized by an image containing a vision of its own excellence (a tyrannizing image).

2. While the content and form of a given culture's tyrannizing image is a product of its past history, current consensus, and future vision, the power or capacity of that image to gain adherence and regulate action is created and sustained in and through cultural communication processes.

3. A culture's ability to integrate and homologize the ideas and actions of individuals is dependent upon its capacity to employ communication to resolve problems of alignment, meaning, and form through ritual, myth, and social drama.

4. Three broad shifts in alignment, meaning, and form are cited as evidence of our culture's declining power over its members and their interpersonal relationships, producing a challenge to our culture's myths, rituals, and social dramas, as illustrated in the regulation of marital relationships in America.

5. It is by examining the cultural myths, rituals, and social dramas designed to regulate the marital process that we obtain our clearest vision of cultural communication at work in balancing individual and collective interests in influencing interpersonal relationship processes.

6. In the traditional marital relationship, the locus of control for solving problems of alignment, meaning, and form are embedded in communal interests resulting in a culture having considerable power over its members and their marital relationships.

7. The advent of a contemporary alternative to traditional marital relationship means that the locus of control for solving problems of alignment, meaning, and form has shifted away from the culture's tyrannizing image toward the individual's ideal self-concept.

8. Because traditional and contemporary marital relationships contain problems of alignment, meaning, and form, a culturally sanctioned myth, ritual, and social drama has emerged which has as one of its principal function the resolution of such conflicts in interpersonal relationships.

9. Regardless of type of marital relationship, traditional or contemporary, interpersonal communication functions as work necessary to self-definition and relationship development.

Note

1. Portions of this chapter rely heavily on the analysis provided by Philipsen, G., "The Prospect For Cultural Communication," Unpublished paper, East West Center, Honolulu, Hawaii, 1981, and Katriel, T., and Philipsen, B., "What We Need is Communication: Communication as a Cultural Category in Some American Speech, *Communication Monographs*, 1981 48, 4:301–318.

References

Berger, P., Berger, B., and Kellner, A. *The Homeless Mind: Modernization and Consciousness.* New York: Vintage, 1974.

Blood, R., and Blood, M. Amicable divorce. *Alternative Lifestyles.* 2, 483–98, Nov. 1979.

Hacker, A. Divorce à la Mode. *New York Review of Books.* 23–30. May, 1979.

Katriel, T., and Philipsen G. What we Need is Communication: Communication as a Cultural Category in Some American Speech. *Communication Monographs*, 48 (4):301–318, 1981.

Levi-Strauss, C. *The Anthropologist as Hand*, eds. E. Neison Hayes and Tanya Hayes, Cambridge, Mass: M.I.T. pp. 145–50, 1970.

Newsweek, 73–76. July 31, 1981.

Philipsen, G. The Prospect for Cultural Communication. Unpublished paper presented at seminar on Communication Theory for Eastern and Western Perspectives. East West Center, Honolulu, HI, 1981.

Sennett, R. *The Fall of Public Man: On the Social Psychology of Capitalism.* New York, NY: Vintage, 1976.

Steiner, G. *Language and Silence: Essays on Language, Literature and the Inhuman.* 1967.

Swensen, C., Eskew, R., and Kohlhepp, K. Stages of Family Life-Cycle, Ego Development and Marital Relationship. *Journal of Marriage and the Family* Vol. 43, 841–52, 1981.

Tamashiro, R. Developmental Stages in the Conceptualization of Marriage. *Family Coordinator.* 27, 238–45, 1978.

Turner, V. Social dramas and stories about them. *Critical Inquiry.* 19, 141–68, 1980.
Vaughan, D. Uncoupling. *Alternative Lifestyles.* 2, pp. 415–42. Nov. 1979.
Weaver, R. *Vision of Order: The Cultural Crises of Our Time*, Baton Rouge. LA: LSU
    Press, 1964.

9
Cross-Cultural Communication and Interpersonal Relationships

> Cultures exist primarily to create and preserve common sys-
> tems of symbols by which their members can assign and exchange
> meanings. Unhappily, the distinctive rules that govern these
> symbol systems are far from obvious. About some of these codes,
> such as language, we have extensive knowledge. About others,
> such as gestures and facial codes, we have only rudimentary
> knowledge. On many others . . . rules governing topical appro-
> priateness, customs regulating physical contact, time and space
> codes, strategies for the management of conflict . . . we have
> almost no systematic knowledge.
>
> D. Barnlund (1975:7-8)

Communication between People from Different Cultural Groups

Increased mobility and access to the means of communication have made most
Americans aware that their self-concepts are different from the self-concepts of
people in other cultures. In the United States alone, over 20 million people visit
from abroad each year (Samovar, Porter and Jain 1981). Tourists, businessmen,
government officials, educators, students and athletes from America visit other
countries each year. When we add to this the large number of intercultural marriages and friendships which develop from such visits, it becomes apparent that
most Americans will spend some time, and some Americans a great deal of time,
in interaction with people from other cultures.

Above and beyond the problem of acquiring a common language, establishing,
maintaining, and terminating interpersonal relationships at the cross-cultural level
of interaction present the individuals involved with one very important problem.
The consensus mechanisms by which communicators function as active participants
in their respective cultures are unique to each culture. Thus both communicators
must, if they are to understand and establish interpersonal relationships with one
another, come to grips with their own cultural roles and with the cultural rules of
those with whom they interact. Such reciprocal responsibilities do not normally
arise when one communicates within one's own culture. Nor are these responsibilities easy to fulfill. How does a person in one culture indicate to a person from
another the cultural pressures that govern his or her self-object relationships?

Similarly, how does a person in one culture discover the cultural inclinations conveyed by the communication of a person from another culture?

Fortunately, there is a way to deal with the problems involved in communication across cultures. It is our position that control over this process comes from bringing to conciousness our own cultural tendencies or assumptive world views and those of others, and then defining the conventions that link what is perceived with what is communicated. It is the purpose of this chapter to clarify this process by examining the assumptive world view and conventions that link what is perceived with what is communicated in regard to (1) interpersonal communication between friends and mates and (2) organizational communication between supervisors and subordinates and decision makers in two divergent cultures.

The extent to which culture affects communication between people from different cultural groups is a function of the dissimilarity between the cultures, rules, or self-concepts (Samovar, Porter and Jain 1983). As we indicated in the previous chapter, culture is a socialization process that influences one's self-concept or the way we relate to objects, other persons, and places. The extent of the difference in self-object relationships between members of two cultural groups depends on the uniqueness of each's socialization process. Two of the most divergent cultural traditions of mankind are the Eastern tradition associated with such countries as Japan, China, India, and Korea, and the Western tradition associated with such countries as the United States, Great Britain, Italy, Germany, and France. We shall select Japan and the United States as representatives of these divergent traditions and examine the problems involved in cross-cultural communication between people in these diverse cultures at (1) the interpersonal and (2) the organizational levels of interaction.

Interpersonal Communication in Japan and the United States

Interpersonal communication in Japanese and American cultures differs, according to Naotsuka and Sakamoto (1981). In Japan most interactional occasions call for the ritualistic use of explicit statements of politness, while there is a comparative lack of formalities in the United States. These differences are due to a Japanese emphasis on mutual dependence, self-depreciation, and use of mutual apology as a social lubricant to conversation. In America we tend to be mutually independent, self-asserting, and likely to employ confrontation as a lubricant for social interaction.

Mutual dependence vs. mutual independence. For the Japanese, interaction, activities, and accomplishments are viewed in terms of a group effort or of a dependence on others. Therefore, one is expected to demonstrate in communication an explicit awareness of others, their social status, and contribution to group harmony. For Americans, interaction, activities, and accomplishments are viewed as individual achievements. Members of a group are regarded as independent individuals in a voluntary, temporal association of equals.

Self-depreciation vs. self-assertion. The Japanese value self-depreciation as a sign of recognizing their cultural or group place. One should not stand out, but

demonstrate through communication that one has no selfish delusions of independent grandure. For Americans the opposite is the case. They value self-assertion,
independence, and the importance of demonstrating through communication who
they are and what they can do.

   Mutual apology vs. mutual confrontation as a social lubricant to interaction.
Japanese employ mutual apology as the chief technique for encouraging interaction
and for keeping things running smoothly. One is always expected to begin with an
apology and respond to any awkwardness, regardless of personal responsibility,
with an apology. Americans seldom apologize and encourage the smooth flow of
interaction by confronting others in regard to their attitudes, values, and beliefs,
as well as the evidential basis for those values and beliefs. Such confrontations
invite and receive a response from others.

   The communication of personal opinion is handled quite differently in each
culture. In Japan personal opinions are avoided, and, when forced to present them,
the Japanese convey them indirectly and implicitly through subtle nuances in tone
and phrasing which rely on cultural resonance or non-verbal cues. In contrast,
Americans are usually ready to express a personal opinion directly and frankly.
These differences are due to the Japanese value of avoiding confrontation, avoiding
personal explanations, and avoiding anything that will separate them out from the
group. Americans thrive on and value direct confrontation, verbal explanations,
and expressions of personal inclination.

   Friendship and mate selection represent two of the most interpersonally intimate
communication activities in any culture. Extensive research has been conducted
on these interaction processes by scholars in Japan and the United States. Let's
explore each in turn for similarities and differences. In so doing, we shall gain
an insight into the problems and prospects for cross-cultural relationships in these
areas.

Friendship in Japan and the United States

Atsumi (1980) maintains that the Japanese form two types of friendships: (1) *tsukiai*,
or interpersonal relationships cultivated and maintained as a result of social obligation, and (2) *friends*, or close interpersonal relationships that develop from
mutual liking, attraction, interest, or common values. Interpersonal relationships
based on social obligation or *tsukiai* are usually tied to work or neighborhood
contacts of limited duration. Interpersonal relationships based on mutual liking,
attraction, interests, or values, or *friends*, are usually among same sex schoolmates
and usually last a life time. Opposite-sex friends, according to Mochizuki (1981),
are rare, with 20% of his survey reporting no known opposite sex friends prior to
their engagement. Atsumi reports that the number of close friends one has is small,
but these friends serve the important function of allowing one to talk freely about
a broad range of mutual interests while being at ease. Japanese close interpersonal
relationships are thus divided between those necessary for work and those rooted
in common interests. Friendship interpersonal relationships tend to be with others
of the same sex, are small in number, and allow for intimate interaction in which
one feels at ease.

Recall that back in Chapter Four we summarized the current state of research on the friendship formation process in the United States. There we discovered that friendship is based on common ideal and real values, authenticity or honesty and trust, and upon social/psychological support. We further noted that Americans frequently classify friendship relations along a dimension which includes social acquaintances, good friends, close friends, and best friends. Friendship was further classified into two roles, confidant and companion. A confidant is someone who respects and supports an individual's evaluative self-object relationships, while a companion is someone who supports an individual's behavioral self-object relationships. Americans tend to have numerous acquaintances, close and good friends from both sexes, but only a small number of best friends. American best friend relationships tend to involve both sexes, to be small in number, to be rooted in common interests, and to allow for evaluative and behavioral self-concept support.

While several studies have been conducted comparing Japanese and American friendship patterns, two are of particular interest to our present analysis. Takahara (1974) undertook a comparative study of Japanese and American synonyms for friendship. Thirty subjects from each culture evenly divided by sex listed the following terms with the highest frequencies:

Japan	(n)	America	(n)
1. Togetherness	25	1. Understanding	29
2. Trust	24	2. Respect	25
3. Warmth	23	3. Sincerity	24
4. Understanding	19	4. Trust	22
		Togetherness	22
		Helping	22
		Caring	22

Note the similarity in the two lists in regard to togetherness, trust, warmth, caring, and understanding. Gudykunst and Nishida (1983) explored similarities and differences in regard to Japanese and American friendships focusing on the degree and scope of their social penetration on specific topics of interaction. They found similarities in 16 out of 37 comparisons. The differences which emerged follow. Americans tend to talk more often and to penetrate deeper into such topics as marriage, love/dating/sex, and emotions. Japanese tend to talk more often about interests/hobbies, school/work, biographical matters, religion and money issues. They also tend to talk more about physical activities and to achieve greater social penetration on this topic.

In short, while Japanese and American friendships are very similar in regard to focus and function, they differ in regard to the male/female ratios of friendship and the topics of conversation. Americans tend to be more concerned with marriage, love/dating/sex, and emotion, while the Japanese are more concerned with physical activities, hobbies, work, religion and money issues.

Attention is now directed to an analysis of the mate selection process in both cultures.

Mateship in Japan and the United States

Japanese men marry between the ages of 25 and 28 while women do so between 23 and 25. There are two distinct types of mate selection processes in Japan, marriages which are arranged and those based on love. Seventy-five percent of the marriages follow the arranged pattern, 25% the love pattern. However, 50% of the men who were married reported that they married for love (*Japan Times* 1983). Mochizuki (1981) provides a detailed study of the two mate selection processes in Japan. Each of these mate selection patterns proceeds through three stages: (1) going steady, (2) getting engaged, and (3) marriage. There are some major differences regarding the length of time spent in each stage for each pattern. For arranged marriages the mean length of time from initial date to going steady was two months, initial date to engagement four months, and initial date to marriage five months. For love marriages the mean length of time from initial date to going steady was four months, initial date to engagement 12 months, and initial date to marriage 26 months. In terms of frequency and intimacy of interaction, 75% of both groups report dating more than once a week after the engagement, while 30% of the arranged marriages and 60% of the love relationships report being involved in premarital sex. The average number of close friends of the opposite sex prior to marriage was 3.5 for males and 2.7 for females. Twenty percent of the men reported their wives as their only friend of the opposite sex prior to marriage. Measures of consensus between partners on five topics ranging from where to live to how many children the family should have, yielded consensus in only 7.9% of the cases. These findings indicate that Japanese mate selection tends to vary in length of time and intimacy of interaction according to marital pattern; the quality of interaction seems to be relatively low in regard to the five topics considered; and 20% of the men selected mates from a sample of one.

Recall that back in Chapter Four we reviewed the current literature on the mate selection process in the United States. There we discovered that mateship is based on intelligence, physical attraction, and sex appeal and one's conformity to the other's view of what constitutes an ideal mate. We also discovered that progress through the mate selection process was a function of the lack of discrepancies between the male's real and ideal self and of reciprocated self-concept support. Recall that back in Chapter Five we reported that most Americans viewed love as an antecedent for sex and that 80% of married couples reported participating in premarital sex prior to marriage. We also discovered that most engaged couples think they are in consensus on intimate topics when in fact they are not. Thus, we can conclude that American mate selection tends to involve a single pattern of love and physical attraction based on perceived similarities in intelligence, physical attraction, and sex appeal as well as considerable concern for the stability of the male as reflected in real-ideal self-concept similarity, and that sexual intimacy seems to be high and consensus low in such relationships.

Several important studies have been conducted comparing the Japanese and American mate selection processes. Takahara (1974) undertook a comparative study of Japanese and American synonyms for marriage. Thirty subjects from each culture evenly divided between the sexes reported the following terms with the highest frequency.

Japan	(n)	America	(n)
1. Trust	27	1. Love	30
2. Family	20	2. Respect	27
3. Understanding	18	3. Responsibility	24
4. Problem sharing	17	4. Understanding	23
5. Compromise	17	5. Helping each other	22
6. Love	16	6. Problem sharing	22
7. Endurance	16	7. Trust	21
8. Children	16	8. Encouraging	21

Cushman and Nishida (1984) examined each culture's views of an ideal mate. The following qualities emerged in order of importance by sex:

Japan

M	F
1. Common values	1. Sound health
2. Easy to talk to	2. Honest
3. Sound health	3. Easy to talk to
4. Intelligent	4. Common Values
5. Affectionate	5. Intelligent
6. Honest	6. Affectionate
7. Handles money well	7. Handles money well

America

M	F
1. Sex Appeal	1. Sex Appeal
2. Respect	2. Affectionate
3. Affectionate	3. Respect
4. Supportive	4. Intelligent
5. Friendship	5. Friendship
6. Intelligent	6. Supportive
7. Attractive	7. Attractive

Note the considerable similarity among males and females in both cultures in regard to their conceptions of marriage and ideal mates. However, there are some major differences between the sexes in ranking those qualities. Japanese men seem to be more concerned with common values and affection, while Japanese women focus more on good health and honesty. American men are more concerned with affection, support, and friendship, while American women are more concerned with intelligence. Finally notice the considerable differences between Japanese and Americans in regard to an ideal mate: the Japanese require common values, sound health, and handling money well, while Americans seek sex appeal, physical attraction, and friendship. In short, there appear to be significant cultural differences between the Japanese and Americans in regard to the mate selection process itself, to some of the qualities of marriage, to many of the qualities of an ideal mate and, in particular, to the role love and sex are to play in marriage vs. good health, endurance, money, and children.

What then can we conclude regarding problems of communication arising from cultural differences in the friendship and mate selection processes in these two countries? First, it appears that prospects for establishing cross-cultural friendships may be improved, by respecting cultural differences in regard to the scope of topics appropriate for discussion and the social penetration of these topics. Americans must minimize topics such as marriage, love/sex/dating, and emotions when communicating with Japanese. In turn, Japanese must minimize physical fitness and work when communicating with Americans. Prospects for trouble-free communication in regard to cross-cultural mateship are much less optimistic. Here several cultural barriers appear important. The American preoccupation with love and sex will create problems for the Japanese, and the Japanese concern for good health, children, and endurance will create problems for Americans. Thus, considerable caution is required between Japanese and American persons considering marriage.

Attention is now directed to an examination of cross-cultural similarities and differences between Japan and the United States in regard to organizational communication and interpersonal relationships.

Organizational Communication in Japan and the United States

Organizations come in many different sizes and shapes in both Japan and the United States. Similarly, organizational communication in these organizations involves a variety of activities and varies considerably according to each. Since it is not possible to examine all organizations nor all types of communication within organizations in one small section of this book, we shall restrict our analysis (1) to a consideration of large organization and (2) to such tasks as supervisor-subordinate communication and the process of decisionmaking.

Between 1970 and 1983 large Japanese corporations have come into world prominence in such areas as electronics, autos, computers, steel, industrial chemicals, and film. In fact, Japanese and American corporations rank among the most productive in the world in those areas. Ouchi (1981) provides a suggestive list of contrasts between the Japanese and American models of large organizations.

Japanese	American
1. Lifetime employment	1. Short term employment
2. Slow evaluation and promotion	2. Rapid evaluation and promotion

Japanese	American
3. Non-specialized career paths	3. Specialized career paths
4. Implicit control mechanism	4. Explicit control mechanisms
5. Collective decision making	5. Individual decision-making
6. Collective responsibility	6. Individual responsibility
7. Holistic concern	7. Segmented concern

Let us explore in some detail how these differences manifest themselves in su-pervisors-subordinate communication and in decision-making. *Supervisor-subordinate communication.* Yoshikawa (1982) provides an in depth analysis of the communication differences between Japanese and American corporations. He does this by first examing the cultural values in Japan which form the basis for the difference and then contrasting Japanese and American communication patterns which follow from the values. Four such values are highlighted.

First, the orientation of the Japanese culture is such that it is better to be harmonious than right or frank, and to achieve this end people will do everything to avoid appearing to oppose anyone directly. This value leads to a difference between Japanese and American supervisors. A Japanese manager has as his primary goal to be an effective mediator, the American manager an effective leader. A Japanese manager makes a key distinction between *tatemae* and *honne*. The former means in front; the latter means behind the scenes. In Japanese corporations, differences are handled behind the scenes, while commonalities are the only points of consideration at collective meetings. It goes without saying that at most organizational meetings in America it is the task of the manager to encourage an open and frank confrontation of competing ideas.

Second, the orientation of the Japanese culture is such that it prefers an affective communication style, while Americans prefer an instrumental communication style. The Japanese concentrate on how something is said, the Americans on what is being said. The Japanese supervisor tends to worry about the attitudes and feelings of his subordinates. The Japanese thus have plannned informal get-togethers at bars or *otsukiai* where the chief task of the interaction is to get better acquainted. In America, supervisors seldom go out with subordinates, and when they do it is in addition to work. In *otsukiai* a subordinate can express all his concerns and oppositions, and the supervisor will listen and not use them against him, but rather will use them to further the interests of the subordinate involved.

Third, the orientation of the Japanese culture is to mistrust verbal language, the American culture to equate trust with living up to one's verbal commitments. Accordingly, 76% of Japanese believe a "silent man rather than an eloquent man will be the most successful" (Klopf et al. 1978). A good supervisor is thus a man of few words in Japan. A good supervisor in America defines rules and tasks clearly and gives frequent commands and evaluations.

Fourth, the orientation of the Japanese culture is to employ indirect-intermediate communication, while the Americans prefer a direct style. The Japanese find it very difficult and uncomfortable to talk face to face. They need something in between, whether it be *Otsukiai* or drink or lunch or sports activities such as golf. The Japanese also make extensive use of intermediaries, people who speak for them because they know better the person with whom they have to talk. American managers prefer a direct style and would seldom ask another subordinate to talk to someone rather than to talk themselves on important matters.

Harmony, personal concern, silence, and indirect intermediaries are all characteristics of Japanese supervisor-subordinate communication. Conflict, task-orientation, assertive, and direct communication are characteristics of American supervisor-subordinate communication. Cross-cultural organizational communication between Japanese and American supervisors and subordinates thus becomes very troublesome. American subordinates view Japanese supervisors as lacking direction, being uncommunicative and indirect, and always avoiding conflict. Japanese subordinates view American supervisors as conflict prone, overbearing, talkative, and too direct. We turn now to Japanese and American differences in regard to organizational decision-making.

Organizational Decision-Making

Perhaps no one organizational communication activity is more characteristic of an organization's values than the manner in which it makes decisions. Okabe (1983) provides an in-depth analysis of differences between decision-making in large Japanese and American firms. Japanese organizations seek and obtain consensus before moving on policy decisions. The Japanese assume that differences of opinion can and will be resolved by a rather slow, cumbersome, and roundabout route. Preferably, the Japanese avoid decisions if they can, for the sake of maintaining group harmony. Making a decision always involves resolving conflicts and the idea of conflict and confrontation represent a serious break in the Japanese values of harmony and interdependence. However, when decisions must be made they employ the unique methods of *nemawashi*, the *ringi* system, and *go-betweens*.

Nemawashi is a method for involving all relevant parties in the decision. *Nemawashi* or "root building" refers to binding the roots of a plant before pulling it out of the ground so the main root will strengthen itself prior to dislodgement. The process involves a one-on-one consultation before taking action. This allows each individual or group time to: (1) become aware of the emerging consensus and adjust to it, (2) understand the goals and rationale for the decision, and (3) allow for modifications. Through this method of behind-the-scene negotiation, the group is placed in a position to support the final solution in an open meeting.

Ringi is a system of reverential inquiry about superiors' intentions. This involves the wide circulation of a document to which large numbers of persons affix their signature as a sign of approval. Everyone must approve the proposal before a meeting is held.

Go-betweens are employed to avoid confrontation and to maintain group solidarity. In delicate interactions a neutral person seeks out the opinion of both sides in a conflict and attempts to resolve differences or to terminate discussion without loss of face on either side.

The strategies of *nemawashi, ringi,* and *go-betweens* are behind-the-scenes approaches to conflict resolution aimed at obtaining a public consensus while maintaining group harmony.

Decision-making in American organizations is usually based on an open and frank confrontation of alternative positions, an attempt to resolve conflicts, and then either a vote based upon majority rule, or else a decision by the supervisor. Americans prefer a rational, specific, issue-oriented strategy. Decision-making is something not to be avoided but to be looked forward to as a means for making progress.

Japanese and American organizational decision-making differ in regard to speed, directness, and affect orientation, and in their methods for resolving conflicts and criteria for decision-making (consensus vs. majority rule). All of these differences create cross-cultural communication problems.

What can we conclude from our review of communication in Japanese and American organizations? Harris and Moran (1979:296), who deal with the problem of managing cultural differences when Japanese and American businessmen attempt to make a deal, suggest that we keep the following in mind:

1. Saving face and achieving harmony are more important factors in business dealings for the Japanese, than achieving higher sales and profits.

2. Third party introductions are important. They prefer this indirect approach whereby you utilize a go-between or arbitrator who may be involved until the conclusion of the negotiation.

3. Whomever you approach in the organization, do so at the highest level; the first person contacted is also involved throughout the negotiation.

4. Avoid direct communication on money; leave this to the go-between or lower echelon staff.

5. Never put a Japanese in a position where he must admit failure or impotency.

6. Don't praise your product or services; let your literature or go-between do that.

7. Use business cards with your titles, preferably in both Japanese and English.

8. The logical, cognitive or intellectual approach to them is insufficient; the emotional level of communication is considered important (e.g., as in dealing with a known business associate vs. a stranger).

Cross-cultural communication is important because it conditions our understanding of our own and others' cultures and of our own and others' unique self-concepts. This brief comparison between Japan and the United States helps to illustrate how such an awareness can expand our choice of cultural influence (some people do choose to change cultures) and our choice of individual self-object relationships (some people adopt new sets of personal values). While the similarities between Japanese and American cultures appear small and the differences appear large, particularly in regard to mateship, supervisor-subordinate relationships, and organizational decision-making, knowledge of the similarities and differences involved allows the actor in such situations to exert some measure of control over his or her communication behavior and thus become more effective in establishing, maintaining, and terminating interpersonal relationships. It is in this insight that the importance of communication and its effect upon interpersonal relationships reside in cross-cultural contexts.

Propositions

1. Americans spend increased time in interaction with people from other cultures, and, as a result, they must become aware of their own cultural inclinations and those of the people with whom they interact.

2. We can bring to consciousness our own cultural tendencies and those of others, define the conventions that link what is perceived with what is communicated, and then exert some control over the process of cross-cultural communication.

3. We can clarify the process of cross-cultural communication by examining conventions that link what is perceived to what is communicated in regard to interpersonal communication between friends and mates and to organizational communication between supervisors and subordinates in two divergent cultures.

4. The extent of difference in self-object relationships between members of two cultural groups depends on the uniqueness of each's socialization; the differences between the cultural traditions of Japan, as representative of Eastern traditions, and of the United States as representative of Western traditions, present a representative study of cross-cultural communication.

5. Japanese interactions emphasize mutual dependence, self-depreciation, and mutual apology in a general context of remaining within the group; American interactions emphasize independence, self-assertion, and confrontation in a general context of asserting individuality.

6. While Japanese and American friendships are similar in focus and function, they differ in male/female ratios of friendship and in topics of conversation.

7. Significant cultural differences exist between Japanese and Americans in regard to mate selection itself, to some qualities of marriage, to many qualities of an ideal mate, and to the role love and sex play, in contrast to good health, endurance, money, and children.

8. Prospects for cross-cultural friendships improve by respecting cultural differences in regard to the scope of topics appropriate for discussion and to the social penetration of these topics.

9. Japanese supervisor-subordinate communication is characterized by harmony, personal concern, silence, and indirect intermediaries; in problematical contrast, American supervisor-subordinate communication is characterized by conflict, task-orientation, assertiveness, and direct communication.

11. Japanese and American organizational decision-making differ in regard to speed, directness, orientation on an issue, the methods of resolving conflicts, and criteria for decision-making.

12. Awareness of our own and others' unique self-concepts influences our choice of cultural influences and our choice of individual self-object relationships.

13. Knowledge of similarities and differences involved allows one to exert some measure of control over one's communication behavior and thus become more effective in establishing, maintaining, and terminating relationships.

References

Atsumi, R. Patterns of Personal Relationships. *Social Analysis*. 5, (6):63–78, 1980.

Barnland, D. *Public and Private Self in Japan and the United States: Communicative Styles in Two Cultures*. Forest Grove, OR: International Scholarly Book Services, Inc., 1975.

Cushman, D., and Nishida, T. Mate Selection the United States and Japan. Unpublished manuscript, 1984.

Gudykunst, W., and Nishida, T. Social Penetration and Japanese and American Close Friendships. In *Communication Yearbook*, Vol. 7, ed. R. Bostrom, 1983.

Hall, E. *Beyond Culture*. New York, NY: Anchor Press, 1976.

Harris, Philip R., and Moran, Robert T. *Managing Cultural Differences*. Houston, TX: Gulf, 1979.

Husbands Should be Older than Wives: Poll. *Japan Times*. July 24, 1983.

Klopf, D., Ishii, S., and Cambra, R. How Communicative are the Japanese?. *The Hawaii Times*. July 6, 1978.

Mochizuki, T. Changing Patterns of Mate Selection. *Journal of Comparative Family Studies*. 12 (3), 318–328, 1981.

Naotsuka, R., and Sakamoto, N. *Mutual Understanding of Different Cultures*. Tokyo, Japan: Taishukan Pub. Co., 1981.

Okabe, R. Cultural Assumptions of Communication Theory from Eastern and Western Perspectives: The Case of Japan and the United States. In W. B. Gudykinst (ed.), *International and Intercultural Communication Award*, Vol.7, ed. W. B. Gudykinst. Annandale, VA: Speech Com. Assoc., 1983.

Ouchi, W. *Theory Z*. Reading, MA: Addison-Wesley, 1981.

Saito, M. Nemawashi. *Et Cetera*. 39:205–218, 1982.

Samovar, L., Porter, R., and Jain, N. *Understanding Inter-cultural Communication*. Belmont, CA: Wordsworth, 1981.

Takahara, N. Semantic Concepts of Marriage, Work, Friendship and Foreigner in Three Cultures. In *Intercultural Encounters With Japan*. eds. J. Condon and M. Saito. Tokyo, Japan: Simul Press, 1974.

Yoshikawa, M. Japanese and American Modes of Communication and Implications For Managerial and Organizational Behavior. Unpublished paper, Second International Conference on Communication Theory: Eastern and Western Perspective. Yokohama, Japan., July, 1982.

10

Telecommunications and Interpersonal Relationships

> In preindustrial societies . . . still the condition of most of
> the world today . . . the labor force is engaged overwhelmingly
> in the extractive industries: mining, fishing, forestry, agriculture.
> Life is primarily a game against nature—Industrial societies . . .
> principally those around the North Atlantic littoral plus the Soviet
> Union and Japan . . . are goods-producing societies. Life is a
> game against fabricated nature—A post-industrial society is based
> on services. Hence, it is a game between persons.
>
> Daniel Bell (1973:126–7)

Telecommunications, Interpersonal Relationships, and Post-Industrial Society

Telecommunications is the head and heart of Bell's post-industrial society or
information age. It is one new and important aspect of modern society, the soul
of a future-oriented and consumer-oriented nation. Telecommunications is the home
of radio with its broadcast networks and their affiliates, television with its networks
and cable competitors, motion picture producers and their theatre and television
outlets, videocassettes and discs, news syndicates with their radio, TV, and newspaper outlets, and record production companies with their music store, radio, and
cable television outlets. It is the home of telephonic communications with its labs,
telephone equipment, and services, computers with their business, governmental,
education, and personal applications, and satellites with their microwave systems.
When one thinks of telecommunications, many familiar names immediately come
to mind: CBS, Warner Brothers, RCA, IBM, and AT&T with scores of others. The
interesting new development is that the convergence of what were formerly separate
industrial sectors into a highly interdependent and gigantic telecommunications
colossus is having far reaching, complex, and multifaceted effects on national and
international political, economic, and social order. According to Naisbitt,

> Now, more than 100 years after the creation of the first data communication
> devices, we stand at the threshold of a mammoth communication revolution.
> The combined technologies of the telephone, computer, and television have
> merged into an integrated information and communication system that trans-
> mits data and permits instantaneous interactions between persons and com-

puters. As our transportation network carried the products of industrialization in the past, so too will this emerging communications network carry the new products of the information society. This new integrated communication system will fuel the information society the way energy . . . electricity, oil, nuclear . . . kept the industrial society humming and the way natural power . . . wind, water, and brute force . . . sustained agricultural society.

(Naisbitt 1982: 23–24)

The field of telecommunications owes its importance, potential, and popularity to the convergence of (1) data processing and storing, with its inexpensive, small microprocessors that produce distortion-free digital information and (2) electronic transmission with its inexpensive, world-wide microwave, satellite, and cable linkages (McGillem and McLauchan 1978). These developments mean that many homes may soon be linked to satellites by direct broadcasting, a linkage in which a family work station consisting of a personal computer, telephone, and interactive (two-way) television will provide the means for home entertainment, home information services, and remote shopping (Fombrun and Astley 1982).

In previous chapters, we analyzed communication systems by characterizing human communication as being influenced by the information we have regarding our relationships to objects, along with our attempts to sustain our preferred self-concepts in human interaction. Since we develop an awareness of ourselves as "objects" in the world only by adopting the perspective of others toward ourselves and because our self-concepts form the basis for our communication behavior, we take the position that the self-concept is a product of information obtained through social interaction. When one of our primary sources for obtaining, testing, and storing the information we have about our relationships to objects becomes human-created technology, then an analysis of that technology is required in order to understand how it influences our perceptions of our own self-object relationships and our relationships with others.

What happens to interpersonal relationships when technology is introduced into human communication processes? The purpose of this chapter is to examine the function of telecommunication in the process of self-validation and in the development of interpersonal relationships. To this end, we will (1) discuss trends in social and technological interface in general, and (2) examine in more detail changes that may have to take place in teacher-student and supervisor-subordinate interpersonal relationships. Thus, this chapter aims at a more complete under-standing of the relationship between telecommunications and society as it relates to human communication processes and interpersonal relationships.

Telecommunications: Bridging the Gap between Man and Machine

The field of telecommunications today is a response to the convergence of two technological trends, the growth of efficient data storage and processing and the increasing interlinkages of electronic transmission systems. But its future depends on a trend that is social, human, and interpersonal. In this section, we will take a look at the interface of telecommunications and interpersonal communication. In the following sections, we will extend our analysis to the special role telecommunications plays in the process of self-validation and the development of interpersonal relationships.

Information Theory: Designing people out of and back into Communications Technology.

Information theorists with their mathematical formulations for increasing channel capacity and improving the accuracy of information have had a major impact on the field of telecommunications.

> It is in *telecommunication* that a really hard core of mathematical theory has developed; such theory has been evolved over a considerable number of years, as engineers have sought to define what it is that they communicate over their telephone, telegraph, and radio systems. In such technical systems, the commodity which is bought and sold, called *information capacity*, may be defined strictly on a mathematical basis, without any of the vagueness which arises when human beings or other biological organisms are regarded as "communication systems." (Cherry 1957:40)

In information theory, information is not to be confused with meaning. Instead, it refers to what could be transmitted rather than what actually is transmitted from the source to the receiver (Shannon and Weaver 1964). Used in this way, information is rather a measure of uncertainty.

> The real reason that analysis deals with a concept of information which characterizes the whole statistical nature of the information source, and is not concerned with the individual messages (and not at all directly concerned with the meaning of the individual messages) is that from the point of view of engineering, a communication system must face the problem of handling any message that the source can produce. (Shannon and Weaver 1964:14)

In addition to eliminating the subject of meaning from the study of communication, information theorists also viewed human communication in the same way as they viewed machine communication. According to Wiener (1960:16),

> Society can only be understood through a study of the messages and the communication facilities which belong to it; and—in the future development of these messages and communication facilities, messages between man and machines, between machines and man, and between machine and machine, are destined to play an ever-increasing part.

If a machine can be programmed to selectively encode, decode, and systematically process bits of information, then man can be viewed similarly as one who selectively encodes, decodes, and systematically processes bits of information in accordance with internal programs resulting in "output" (behavior) that represents such internal programs. Thus, the computer as a machine, computing languages, and internal programs provide presumably appropriate metaphors for man, social language, and mentalistic concepts, respectively (Vallacher 1980).

The need is great for designing people back into communications technology. Information theorists' attempts to reduce communication to information and men to machines are as informative about human communication as a medical definition (a flat EEG) is for the meaning of death (Cahn and Hanford, 1984). While reductionism in information theory may have its use in the direct application to the technical equipment itself, a broader perspective is necessary when human beings are included in the process of communication. In psychology, where a similar situation exists, a reduction of subjective human experience to objective behavior (behaviorism) has resulted in a parallel neglect of the psyche or the self. This preoccupation has created a psyche-less psychology just as it has produced a selfless communicology (Cahn and Hanford, 1984). While there is a need to consider the subjective, experiential side of human life in psychology, there is a similar need to deal with the meaningful, symbolic side of human communication. As one of our colleagues noted, "A computer is really dumb; it does only what it is told to do. I don't know a single person who does *that*". The problem was that the machine did not know what our friend *intended*. If telecommunication is to retain its importance and popularity it must incorporate a view of science that treats *persons as persons* and it must study human communication as a process going on between *people*.

Before leaving information theory, we should examine briefly a biased view of humans that also needs to undergo review. This bias stems from the identification of noise in the communication process.

> In the process of being transmitted, it is unfortunately characteristic that certain things are added to the signal which were not intended by the information source. These unwanted additions may be distortions of sound—or static—or distortions in shape or shading of picture—, or errors in transmission— All of these changes in the transmitted signal are called *noise*. (Shannon and Weaver 1964:7–8)

The problem is that information theorists view humans as a source of noise in the communication system leading to errors in the accurate transmission and reception of information. People suffer headaches, sickness, injuries, emotions, needs, purposes, and perspectives that function as noise in the communication process (Bittner 1980). Human errors may occur in the encoding, transmission, and decoding stages of the communication process (Senders 1980). But while information theorists have endeavored to design people out of the communication system, this has not been possible. Just as the industrial society has numerous complex systems, from automated assembly lines to shipping and transportation servies, so will the post-industrial society have numerous complex systems ranging from telecommunications networks to information-entertainment services. And people will play an important role in every aspect of this process. We will need people to supervise, safeguard, and change telecommunications systems. In addition, we will need people to invent, refine, improve, and apply telecommunications developments. Finally, and perhaps most importantly, we will need people to use and create new uses for telecommunications equipment and services, whether it is in agriculture, industry, office administration, medicine, or education. The term "user friendly" is a label for a revolutionary new perspective on the role of human beings in the communications process, and is based on the recognition, finally, that technology needs people, in a vital and creative way.

Mass Communication: From Broadcasting to Narrowcasting in Communications Technology

As the term "mass" suggests, mass communication (including televised motion pictures and news services) via the broadcast media (radio and television) is often designed to reach the largest possible number of people. It is not uncommon for a television program to have an audience in the millions. The effect has been a low level of sensitivity to individuals and individual differences by advertising agencies, sponsors, producers, and other mass communicators. Broad concepts of consumers prevail, and programming is purposely bland to please the general public (Bittner 1980).

Developments in telecommunications technology are resulting in trends toward individualization of information and entertainment transmission. First, computer technology permits a distinct and individually tailored adaptation to each of thousands (Naisbitt 1982). Second, information technology permits information diversity. Publicity is given to a downward trend for national network television due to the increasing options of cable and increasing number of subscribers. Just as numerous special interest magazines captured the readership from *Life, Look,* and *Post,* so are numerous cable networks and neighborhood low power TV stations (LPTV) competing with CBS, NBC, and ABC. Cable and LPTV along with videodiscs and electronic news bases have resulted in "narrowcasting," defined as the targeting of information and entertainment to a predefined audience, according to *Video Buyer's Review,* Summer 1982. Narrowcasting is the electronic version of selective mailings and subscription-only magazines.

In addition to more individually tailored information and educational programming, consumers may experience greater control over what information and entertainment they receive. Until recently, authors, producers, and editors decided what to put in newspapers, magazines, radio shows, and television programs, but now consumers decide what to watch and read. According to Naisbitt (1982:26), "Now, with the new technologies, we will create our own packages, experiencing sovereignty over text. It will evolve over a long period of time, but the accumulated impact of people exercising sovereignty over text will undoubtedly have a strong effect on the new society we are shaping."

Just as information theory must design people back into communication systems, so must mass communication move from broadcasting to narrowcasting in its orientation toward the public. There are strong forces making communication technology more people- and individual-centered. If telecommunications is to survive as an important and popular field, it must reverse the trends of earlier years in which attempts were made to design humans out of the system and efforts were made to locate common denominators to broaden the mass appeal of information and programming. To the extent that machines become user friendly and humans invent, refine, and manage communication technologies, telecommunications may permit distinct and individually tailored information and entertainment programming in two-way interactive systems that blend high speed, high fidelity technologies with meaningful, reflective human communicators. If successful, telecommunications will play an increasing role in the process of self-validation and the development of interpersonal relationships. Two types of interpersonal relationships, boss-employee and teacher-student relationships, which are the subject of the next sections, will be among those significantly affected.

Boss-employee Interpersonal Relationships in an Information Age

Telecommunications and related industries comprise one of the largest and most dynamic sectors of the American economy (Chisman 1982). They are the most profitable, most productive, and fastest growing part of our economy. Sometime in the 1980's, the electronic information industries will become a $400 billion business, the largest ever (Naisbitt 1982). IBM is currently the most profitable industrial company in the United States (Greenwald 1983).

Although the post-industrial society will continue to employ some farmers and factory workers, the information related industries will continue to seize a larger share of available workers. Whereas in 1967 only 25% of the GNP was controlled by the information industries, by 1970 half of the US work force was classified as people who handle information and manipulate symbols rather than produce things, and they earned over half of all labor income (Porat 1977). At one time, 90% of our population produced food; now only 3% of Americans work at farming. A similar decline in this century is expected in manufacturing, especially in light of advances in automation and robotics (Cater 1981). The combination of computers and telephones into a gigantic telecommunications industry further propels the United States into the information age (Porat 1978).

In Chapter Seven we discussed the interface between organizations and interpersonal relationships, especially in the contexts of employment interviewing and employee appraisal. In this section, we want to introduce the variable of telecommunications and its impact on boss-employee interpersonal relationships, and take a futuristic look into the information age. Thus, it is the purpose of this section to describe the changing nature of boss-employee interpersonal relationships, and to examine the traditional role of the boss in light of the impact telecommunications is having in our post-industrial society.

The Traditional Industrial Model

Traditionally, boss-employee relationships were geared to the centralized factory model of the industrial age. An obvious example would be Ford Motor Company's huge plant at River Rouge where 100,000 people worked in the 1920's. Ford and other manufacturers required large concentrations of material, capital, plant, and labor, which meant that thousands of workers might have to convene daily at the same place of work. Large numbers of laborers worked more efficiently when organized vertically or hierarchically with a one-way (mass) communication system in which a top person sent information in one direction downward. Hierarchical organization included high specialization on the assembly line, differentiation, clear separation of duties and responsibilities, close supervision of subordinates, respect for authority and loyalty to supervisors, elaborate rules and controls, and impersonality (Goldhaber 1983). Such industries were known for their pressures on workers to conform to the expectations of the organization and for encouraging an assembly line mode of thinking. They were also known for upward movement, stress and tension, defensive behavior, and anxiety. The top-down organization chart and the chain of command were symbols of boss-employee interpersonal relationships in bureaucratic organizations in the industrial age.

The Telecommunications Mode in the Information Age

There are at least three alternative types of boss-employee interpersonal relationships in post-industrial society, depending on whether one works at home, works for a telecommunications service, or works in an information related industry such as Intel or Tandem. The distinguishing feature about many of these jobs is that the business may be more decentralized than the factories of the industrial era. Since many telecommunications services, jobs, and industries do not require large concentrations of material, capital, plant, or labor, greater diversity of boss-employee relationships is possible and encouraged.

Option One. More workers may stay home rather than report at a designated time and place. If one's home is equipped with telecommunications equipment (perhaps only a computer and a telephone), one can store, process, and transmit information in a way that gives access to everyone and everything that is needed to perform the job. Such an arrangement may appeal to some secretaries, clerks, handicapped workers, and those in some aspects of banking and insurance, to name but a few. Pilot projects are underway in Control Data and at the Continental Bank in Illinois (Naisbitt 1982).

Option Two. Because information has value and may be sold, many workers may start their own data, information, telephone, or telecommunications service. Today one can start one's own business with a telephone and a word processor. There is rapid growth of small business listings in marketing and opinion polling, data processing, programming services, travel assistance, finance and credit, telephone services, library and resumé research, home security, telecommunications, computer, and telephone systems sales such as SPRINT and ROTELCOM. The possibilities for starting a small information business are limited only by one's imagination, knowledge, and investment capability.

Option Three. Large numbers of people already work as systems analysts, computer programmers, and telecommunications service technicians. Today America's largest companies such as AT&T, RCA, and IBM employ millions in high tech jobs. Many workers in this industrial sector are encountering a new management style that greatly alters the traditional boss-employee relationships of the factory model. The Intel Corporation, for example, is organized to avoid the traditional bureaucratic hierarchy. At Intel, (1) workers have more than one boss, (2) committee responsibility has replaced sole responsibility, (3) private offices and privileged parking are nonexistent, (4) dress is informal, (5) all employees participate in decision-making processes, and (6) all employees, even the newest, are encouraged to speak out (Lohr 1981). To a traditional bureaucrat, the Intel model may seem chaotic, unstructured, and lacking in clear divisions of responsibility. The new pattern is intended to circumvent assembly line thinking characteristic of the industrial model and to encourage instead initiative and creativity. Hewlett-Packard Company requires managers to report to their own peers to share information and enhance communication (*Business Week*, June 30, 1980). Because of rigid computer control of production, cost, quality, and reporting systems, managers at Tandem computer company are free to concentrate on "people projects" such as employee stock options, flexible working hours, and sabbatical leaves required of all employees every four years (*Business Week*, July 14, 1980). "Quality circles" have become popular (*Business Week*, May 11, 1981) and "Theory Z" is being promoted as *the* management model (Ouchi 1981).[1]

Regardless of which option one chooses, the distinguishing feature is networking, almost a synonym for decentralization, which fosters equality and informality in worker and boss-employee interpersonal relationships. Networking describes people sharing information with each other. This new management style is lateral, diagonal, bottom up, and interdisciplinary (Naisbitt 1982). In contrast to bureaucracies, networks provide the horizontal link. According to Hine (1977), a network may be characterized as "a badly knotted fishnet," but this phrase fails to capture the three-dimensional nature of networks that makes them even more complex. Whether one is in business for oneself, stays at home and works for someone else, or is employed by some information industries, one may find oneself embedded in a network where everyone serves everyone else. Networking captures the essence of the post-industrial society, which is based on services and is a transaction between people.

Teacher-Student Interpersonal Relationships in an Information Age

While there are many signs that telecommunications is popular at home and at work, there are signs that telecommunications may *not* function the same way in the schools and universities, especially in regard to the teaching-learning process and teacher-student interpersonal relationships. Unlike the home situation or work place, there are particular barriers to the widespread use of communications technology in the teaching-learning process in public schools and in state-supported institutions of higher education.

While an exception occurs for limited *computer* applications in some office administrations and in many faculty research and publishing activities, there has been and continues to be far less interest in the application of telecommunications in education, for several reasons (Tucker 1983). First, because educators tend to focus on full time students on campus rather than on part-time students and off-campus courses, they have created standards and policies that impede the use of telecourses. For example, course credit may be earned only for courses in which "a licensed teacher is physically present in the classroom, thus negating any economies that might be achieved through technology" (Tucker 1983:120). Second, because educational use of communications technology depends on public support derived from general taxes, educators who tolerate some use of telecommunications if trouble-free have been quick to cut it when public funding is scarce (Tucker 1983). Third, because traditional educational organizations have very little incentive to increase efficiency and to innovate, educators have *not* encouraged the use of technology that could have the side effects of reducing the size of staff and faculty. As stated by Chisman (1982:75):

> There are many reasons for this laggardly performance by the service sector, but at least one that is highly relevant here is that large parts of it consist either of government itself or of non-profit organizations dependent on government (most education, health, and other public services). Because these institutions have no "bottom line," they have very little incentive to increase productivity, either through technological innovations or in other ways.

Fourth, because educators have used their political influence to deny accreditation and financial support to technology-oriented curricula at public and state supported institutions, private industries are spending increasing amounts on training. For example, IBM and AT&T spend annually $500 million and $1.7 billion respectively on employee training (Naisbitt 1982; Tucker 1983).

Finally, and perhaps most significantly, because educators must adhere to a particular set of budgeting practices that differ greatly from those of private industry, they allocate funds toward proven instructional programs rather than experimental and risky academic ventures such as telecommunications programs. Businesses, on the other hand, are prepared and designed to make substantial investments if they see reasonable likelihood of capital returns:

Some firms, like General Electric, have started to sell their graduate-level education engineering programs to other firms, creating the possibility of educational markets aggregated across firms. Such markets, large enough to warrant substantial investment in courseware, would be ideally suited to telecommunications applications. William Norris, the chief executive officer of Control Data Corporation, has spoken of the interest of the nation's business leaders in "education as a business opportunity" (Tucker 1983:121–122).

While communications technology may have a limited role to play in the teaching-learning process in state- and public-funded educational institutions, we believe nonetheless that the post-industrial society, in which telecommunications is the head and heart, is having and will continue to have a great impact on educators in general and on teacher-student relationships in particular. Thus, in this section, we will describe the changing nature of teacher-student interpersonal relationships and examine the traditional role of the teacher with regard to socio-cultural changes being produced by the information age.

The Traditional Learning Model of the Industrial Era

The traditional educational system was geared to the pre-industrial and industrial societies. For example, the lecture method was indicative of the traditional bureaucratic, top-down, hierarchical structure of traditional industry. According to Tofler 1970:362):

> Yet the whole idea of assembling masses of students (raw material) to be processed by teachers (workers) in a centrally located school (factory) was a stroke of industrial genius. The whole administrative hierarchy of education, as it grew up, followed the model of industrial bureaucracy. The very organization of knowledge into permanent disciplines was grounded on industrial assumptions. Children marched from place to place and sat in assigned stations. Bells rang to announce changes of time. Young people passing through this educational machine merged into an adult society whose structure of jobs, roles and institutions resembled that of the school itself. The school-child did not simply learn facts that he could use later on; he lived, as well as learned, a way of life modelled after the one he would lead in the future.

Most people who recall their days in school remember vividly the invariant organizational structure of the teacher-led classes. Classroom windows were generally to the left of the students as they sat in fixed rows facing a blackboard, large desk, and the teacher dressed rather formally. As one moved up, grade by grade, the student remained in this rigid scheme, gaining no experience with fluid, rapidly changing organizational systems or with substituting one type of organizational form for another different type. In addition, the pattern of movement conformed to the upward mobility in industry and to the "assembly line mode of thought." In a system based on authority, teacher-student relationships were one of dominance vs. submission, informed vs. naive, and active (teacher) vs. passive (students). Thus, in the traditional learning model, one person was viewed as the teacher of facts and skills while the other persons were viewed as a class of students there to be taught.

The New Learning Model in the Information Age

Just as the traditional learning model was geared to the preindustrial and industrial societies, so must the new learning model reflect the changes taking place socially, economically, and politically. We could point to the growing needs for the retraining of workers and the concept of life-long learning, for tutors of individuals in business and consulting services to companies and organizations, for joint ventures by universities and businesses in research and teaching, for short-term learning contracts, for general rather than specialized education of workers, and for abandoning fixed, rigid disciplines and obsolete curricula. Rather than be carried away by predictions about the future of universities and schools, we prefer to deal primarily with the role of the teacher in today's classroom and in the immediate future.

The new learning model is designed to meet the current needs of students in the post-industrial society who are to learn (1) how to cope with rapid change, (2) how to think, make decisions, and solve problems, and (3) how to develop insights and be creative. To meet these needs, teachers must avoid the traditional model of teacher-student relationships which is based on authority and encourages assembly line thinking.

To teach students how to copy with rapid change, teachers must abandon their strict adherence to the lecture method and traditional classroom organization and use variable methods of instruction in a variety of classroom organizations. While the traditional method permits only vertical communication and hierarchical organization which is unidirectional, the new model emphasizes networking in that it features more horizontal communication which is interactive and participatory (Hogrebe 1981). Unfortunately for some innovative teachers, some school and university policies regarding the number and length of classroom meetings, required teacher and/or student classroom attendance, the location of classes, and dress codes for teachers will need to undergo review if teachers are to meet the needs of the new era. Many teachers know how difficult it is to change the location of a single class or to require attendance to some event outside the normal classroom or at a time other than the normal class hour. Today's classroom should be a mixture of inside and outside learning activities, a combination of lectures, class and small group discussions, case studies, on site visits, guest lectures, films or videotapes, a variety of structured and some unstructured games and simulations, and a combination of opportunities to speak and write. In contrast to the classroom of yesterday, in which students expected to sit, take notes, and be taught, today's students should enroll in a course without knowing what to expect. The teacher-student interpersonal relationship will emphasize more equality and informality as the teacher acts more in the role of facilitator of change and of helper in adapting to this change.

To teach students how to think, make decisions, and solve problems, teachers must abandon the practice of basing grades primarily on recall tests. One of the interesting outcomes derived from computer technology is the realization that humans think differently from machines. The computer can store facts, manipulate them logically, and transmit them, but it cannot make decisions as humans can. When people perceive facts, store them, and recall them for a test, they are thinking like a computer and will someday be replaced by one if they continue to think that way. Humans have the unique capacity to abstract and concretize, to use variable logics, manipulate facts and symbols, and to persuade others in a way that a computer cannot. Teachers should exploit this capability by helping students learn how to think, make decisions, and solve problems. Obviously such instruction must include emotional and ethical components. Today, some classroom activites should involve case studies of ethical dilemmas and some questions on tests should consist of word problems to be solved. How one evaluates facts, cultural influences on thought patterns, language and logic, ethics, the nature of man and the meaning of life, and the future and quality of life are a few of the many topics that need attention in the new curriculum. Whereas the teacher of yesterday was the authority and giver of facts and skills, today the teacher causes students to reflect on their values. The teacher-student interpersonal relationship will include a stronger affective component as the teacher occupies more of a role of facilitator of personal emotional growth.[2]

To teach students to be more creative, teachers need to abandon the precept that their way is the only or the right way to cope and think. To create requires the human gift of insight and the ability to look at problems from many and new angles. In essence, it is the process by which we teach ourselves. Tofler (1970:363–364) says that in the post-industrial society

> "fast, fluid and self-regulating-machines will deal with the flow of infor-
> mation and insight. Machines will increasingly perform the routine tasks;
> men the intellectual and creative tasks. The technology of tomorrow requires
> not millions of lightly lettered men, ready to work in unison at endlessly
> repetitive jobs, it requires not men who take orders in unblinking fashion,
> aware that the price of bread is mechanical submission to authority, but men
> who can make critical judgements, who can weave their way through novel
> environments, who are quick to spot new relationships in the rapidly changing
> reality. It requires men, who in C.P. Snow's compelling term, "have the future
> in their bones."

Some classroom activities should include role-playing, experientially-based techniques, brainstorming sessions, and case studies. Teachers should encourage creative, insightful solutions to problems. Inherently creative subjects in the arts should be a part of every student's course of study. Perhaps the greatest skill educators could inspire in the workers of tomorrow is the ability to learn, relearn, and unlearn. While the traditional lecturer embodied the rote-memory approach to learning, today teachers must master the creative process. The teacher-student interpersonal relationship will include an exciting new dimension as the teacher plays a greater role in facilitating the students' creative talents.

Whether or not the teacher desires to change his or her instructional methods and strategies, we believe that the system will produce such changes eventually. There is less awareness and less agreement as to which instructional methods and classroom strategies are also obsolete. At the present, education is in a state of transition but as the information age takes greater hold, we believe that it will become obvious to everyone that there must be changes in the nature of the teacher-student interpersonal relationship. Informality, equality, flexibility, adaptability, creativity will replace the traditional values that encouraged formality, authority, bureaucracy, inflexibility, and the assembly line mode of thinking. As teachers avoid the traditional industrial model of learning and adopt the role of facilitator of personal growth, they will reorient themselves around new educational goals and will better meet the needs of today's and future generations. Teaching students how to cope in a rapidly changing world, how to think, and how to create embodies the spirit of mankind's role in the post-industrial society.

In summary, the convergence of two technologies . . . data processing and storage and electronic transmission . . . is impelling our society into an information age under the rubic of telecommunications. The distinguishing feature of the new era is it dramatically increases the information people have about their relationship to objects, thus bringing together traditionally separate and distinct fields of communications technology and interpersonal communication. Whereas in the past many technological developments were applied to broadcasting and mass communication, in the future the convergence of computer and electronic transmission technologies will be applied to define and redefine our relationship to objects or interpersonal communication. If it is to survive in importance and popularity, the field of telecommunications will have to creatively link information to people and people to information.

Because of values such as profit and efficiency underlying modern business management, private industry is motivated to incorporate large amounts of computer, electronic communications, and telecommunications technology. In addition, private industry can afford sizable investments in a technology that offers reasonable expectations of financial gain. Therefore, telecommunications and related computer and electronic information industries are enjoying considerable popularity in private homes and in private industry, a popularity which in turn is producing an important change in worker and boss roles and their interpersonal relationships. Workers are experiencing more options as to work schedule and work place. A new management style which recognizes the concept of networking features decentralization of authority and responsibilty, informality, service, and a people-orientation. A horizontal communication network is replacing the traditional top down hierarchical communication characteristic of organizations in the industrial era.

Although communications technology is less popular in education than private industry, the post-industrial society in which telecommunications is key will bring economic, political, and social forces to bear on the entire institution of education, resulting in changes in teacher-student interpersonal relationships. As a part of the student learning network, the role of teacher will be less formal and authoritative than previously, and more facilitative in helping students learn for themselves how to cope with rapid change, how to think, how to make decisions, and how to solve problems, and how to gain insight and be creative.

Propositions

1. We stand today on the threshold of an even larger scale communications revolution that will convert the industrial era into an information age that is based primarily on services and transactions between people.

2. The field of telecommunications, which is a response to the convergence of efficient, inexpensive data storage and processing technology and a world-wide network of electronic transmission technology, is the head and heart of the post-industrial society.

3. The future of telecommunications lies in the interface of man and machine, that is, interpersonal communication and communications technology.

4. Whereas in the past information theorists designed humans out of the communications systems because engineers were hesitant to deal with the subject of meaning, viewed man as a machine, and viewed man as the source of noise in the communication process, in the future human beings must be designed back into communications systems if the field of telecommunications is to retain its importance and popularity.

5. Whereas in the past communications technology was applied primarily to broadcasting, in the future it will be applied to narrowcasting and interpersonal communication.

6. Because modern industry stresses efficiency, it is motivated to invest substantially in computer, electronic communications, and telecommunications which in turn will greatly alter the nature of boss-employee interpersonal relationships.

7. The traditional centralized industrial model, which is characterized as a highly rigid, top-down, hierarchical communication system popular in assembly line style factories, is being replaced by a new decentralized telecommunications model which is described as a highly flexible, lateral, diagonal, bottom, up, interdisciplinary network where people serve one another and share information in more equal and informal management styles.

8. Although the technology itself is expected to play less of a role in education than in private industry, the information age will produce economic, social,

and political forces that in turn will greatly alter the nature of teacher student interpersonal relationships.

9. As a part of the student learning network, the role of teacher will be less formal and authoritative than previously and more facilitative in helping students learn for themselves how to cope with rapid change, how to think, make decisions, and solve problems, and how to gain insight and be creative.

Notes

1. "Quality circles" (QC), created by an American quality control expert, W. Edward Deming, but popularized in Japan especially by Nissan and Toyota, operates on the value of worker participation. In groups, workers discuss work-type problems and solutions, on company time. Now enjoying a revival of interest in the United States, quality circles are used regularly in over 200 companies. See "The New Industrial Relations," *Business Week*, May 11, 1981, and *Training/HRD*, August 1980.

Theory Z refers to Ouchi's attempt to combine Japan's holistic management philosophy (lifetime employment, decision by consensus, collective responsibility, etc.) with America's individualized management system (individual responsibility, evaluation and promotion of individuals, specialized career paths, etc.). Although the two management philosophies are quite different, some American companies have successfully integrated some aspects of both the Japanese and American management systems (Naisbitt 1982; Goldhaber 1983).

2. There are at least two trends in teacher education that are of special interest to teachers and students of interpersonal communication. First, there is increasing recognition that communication variables function in the instructional environment as they do in a broader social context (Sorensen 1981). This trend necessitates the investigation of what a teacher both says and does along with students' perception of these words and actions. Second, there is increasing awareness that some therapeutic and counseling variables which also happen to be interpersonal communication constructs operate in teacher-student relationships as they do in professional helping relationships. This trend is resulting in many teachers viewing their role more as that of "helper-teacher" (Gazda 1973). Together, these trends in teacher education encourage teachers to enhance their communcation skills in order to help students resolve their own problems and to communicate to their students nonpossessive warmth, caring, genuineness, acceptance, openness, and respect (Cahn 1983).

References

Bell, D. *The coming of postindustrial society*. New York, NY: Basics, 1973.

Bittner, J.R. *Broadcasting: An introduction*. Englewood Cliffs, NJ: Prentice-Hall, 1980.

Business Week, June 30, 1980.

Business Week, July 14, 1980.

Business Week, May 11, 1981.

Cahn, D.D. The Relative Effects of the Perception of Being Understood/Misunderstood on Teacher-Student Relationships. Paper presented at the summer conference of the International Communication Association, Seoul, Korea, 1983.

Cahn, D.D., and Hanford, J.T. Perspectives on Human Communication Research. *Western Journal of Speech Communication*. 48:277–292, 1984.

Cater, D. The Survival of Human Values. *Journal of Communication*. 31:190–203, 1981.

Cherry, C. *On Human Communication: A Review, a Survey, and a Criticism*. New York, NY: Science Editions, 1957.

Chisman, F.P. Beyond Deregulation: Communications Policy and Economic Growth. *Journal of Communication*. 32:69–83, 1982.

Fombrun, C., and Astley, W.G. The Telecommunications Community: An Institutional Overview. *Journal of Communication*. 32:56–68, 1982.

Gazda, G.M. *Human relations development: A manual for educators*. Boston, MA: Allyn and Bacon, 1973.

Goldhaber, G.M. *Organizational Communication* (3rd edition). Dubuque, IA: W. C. Brown, 1983.

Greenwald, J. The Colossus that Works. *Time*, July 11, 1983.

Hine, V. The Basic Paradigm of a Future Socio-Cultural System. *World Issues*, April-May, 1977.

Hogrebe, E.F.M. Digital Technology: The Potential for Alternative Communication. *Journal of Communication*. 31:170–76, 1981.

Lohr, S. Overhauling America's Business Management. *New York Times Magazine*, January 4, 1981.

McGillem, C.D., and McLauchan, W.P. *Hermes Bound: The Policy and Technology of Telecommunications*. W. Lafayette, IN: Purdue Research Foundation, 1978.

Naisbitt, J. *Megatrends: Ten new directions transforming our lives*. New York, NY: Warner Communications, 1982.

Ouchi, W. *Theory Z*. Reading, MA: Addison-Wesley, 1981.

Porat, M.U. *The information economy: Definition and measurement* (nine volumes). Washington, D.C.: US Government Printing Office, 1977.

Porat, M.U. Global implications of the information society. *Journal of Communication*. 28:70–80, 1978.

Senders, J.W. Is There a Cure for Human Error? *Psychology Today*. April, 1980.

Shannon, C.E., and Weaver, W. *The Mathematical Theory of Communication*. Urbana, IL: University of Illinois, 1964.

Sorensen, G.A. The Relationship Between Teacher's Self-Disclosure Statements and Student Affect. Paper presented at the annual convention of the International Communication Association, Minneapolis. 1981.

Training/HRD, August, 1980.

Tofler, A. *Future Shock*. London: Pan Books, 1970.

Tucker, M.S. The turning point: Telecommunications and higher education. *Journal of Communication*, 33:118–130, 1983.

Vallacher, R.R. An introduction to self theory. In D. M. Wegner & R.R. Vallacher (Eds.), *The self in social Psychology*. Oxford: Oxford University, 1980.

Video Buyer's Review, Summer, 1982.

Wiener, N. *The human use of human beings*. Garden City, N.Y.: Doubleday, 1954.

Postscript

We began this inquiry by suggesting that knowledge of the principles, processes, and skills which follow from four propositions constitute the framework for our unique insights into the problems and processes of communication in interpersonal relationships.

First, from a rules perspective comes the proposition that human communication is guided and governed by socially established rules.

Second, from the symbolic interactionist perspective comes the proposition that who we are, our identity or self-concept, is a symbolic creation formed and sustained in our interaction with others.

Third, from an action theory perspective comes the proposition that our interpersonal relationships are constructed out of different types of reciprocal self-concept support.

Fourth, from a systems perspective comes the proposition that our self-concepts and in turn our interpersonal relationships are significantly influenced by our participation in organizational, cultural, cross-cultural and telecommunications interaction processes.

We have attempted to present the principles and skills required to influence our interpersonal relationships through human communication. However, if we do not choose to master these skills and learn these principles, then we fall prey to the tyrannizing influences of other selves, our work, our culture, others' cultures and technology. It is in this vision of human kind as having the potential to function as active, intentional, human, creative and skilled influencers of their own fate that the unique insight of this work resides. The challenge is not to allow this vision to escape our grasp.

The information we have regarding who we are, is *not* determined socially by whom others think we are, nor is it determined psychologically by whom we think we are. Rather, it is an interactively determined construct formed in interaction with others and based upon our own and other's communication skills. For example, an individual's ability to manifest one's self as intelligent may or may not be sustainable depending on whether others, (1) fail to challenge our assertion of self,

(2) challenge and defeat our assertion of self, or (3) challenge but are overcome by our assertion of self. In short, one's ability to create and sustain our vision of self depends upon the room others provide for us or the room we create in interaction to develop, present and validate our self-concepts.

Author Index

Subject Index